3/92

Love and Glory

Also by Larry Underwood:

The Custer Fight and Other Tales of the Old West.

Love and Glory
Women of the Old West

Larry Underwood

Media Publishing
Lincoln, Nebraska

ISBN 0-939644-79-7
Library of Congress Card Catalog Number 90-63202

Cover design by Angie Johnson

Printed in the United States of America

Media Publishing
A Divison of Westport Publishers, Inc.
2440 'O' Street
Lincoln, Nebraska 68510

To my wife

Beverly Sue Albert Underwood

There is in every true woman's heart
a spark of heavenly fire,
which lies dormant
in the broad daylight of prosperity;

but which kindles up,
and beams and blazes
in the dark hour of adversity.

Washington Irving
The Sketch Book, the Wife

Table of Contents

A Word of Special Thanks

Researching writers owe a great deal to librarians. Some of them we come in contact with, like Mrs. Nancy Moennig at the South County Library, others we never see. They work in dusty stacks looking for books requested through the systems libraries that now crisscross our land.

Researching writers owe a great deal to friends. Don Pierson, Cheyenne, Wyoming's chief of police, was a great help. John Joerschke, editor of *True West*, offered suggestions. A lady in Franklin, Tennessee—the County Historian, provided valuable information. A friend from Illiopolis, Illinois, knew a great deal about the Donner family. Dee Brown's encouragement, as always, inspired me to dig for the facts that would make the women's stories unique. And on and on it goes.

Researching writers owe a great to deal modern transportation. The automobile carried me to the area of Cynthia Ann Parker's birth, to the area where she spent a quarter century as a Comanche wife, and finally, to her burial site at Fort Sill. Visits to Susan Magoffin's last home, the Donner's farm, the site of Frances Grummond's husband's death, the site of Fanny Kelly's rescue, the town of Mary C. Collins' birth, the area of one of Carry Nation's "hatchetations" were all routine trips just a century or so after it took six or seven months to travel the danger-fraught trail from Independence, Missouri to San Francisco.

Researching writers (who are male) owe a great deal to the women in their lives. Very special thanks are due to my wife, my mother, my aunts, my daughters, my teachers, and other friends for the insight they gave me into their role in the formation of this civilization called America.

To Linda Messman, editor and happy Nebraska grandmother, and Sam Smith, a friend who read *Love and Glory* to get rid of those mistakes writers never make, a special thanks.

Larry D. Underwood
Meppen, Illinois
1991

Introduction

The Great American West of the 1800s spread from the lush, primordial forests of the Mississippi River Valley over tallgrass prairies and shortgrass prairies to the vast expanse of the Rocky Mountains. It was a rich, beautiful land and Americans east of the Mississippi were drawn by the riches and the beauty.

The first visitors to this wonderland entered from the northwest tens of thousands of years ago. They came to be called American Indians. Nature guided them, directing them over this land. And from nature, these early people learned to live. They fished the streams and ocean. They hunted the antelope and buffalo. They harvested all of nature's gifts.

Later, when the Europeans came, they arrived in four phases. In the period of discovery, there were explorers who gave way to mountain men. Not far behind them were ox-drawn wagon trains laden with immigrants. Railroads followed and close behind was the slaughter of the buffalo and the resulting Indian Wars. Next came the era of cattle, cowboys, cowtowns and gunslingers. And following that, the influx of farmers. Somewhere in all of this came miners looking for the rich ores the West would give up. And, somewhere in all of this, women moved West.

At first, there were only Indian women in the West. But then, beginning in the 1840s, women from the States began arriving. There were not many. In Denver, Colorado, during that community's founding year, there were less than a half-dozen females from the East.

And when women did come, they had to face the misery and death of frontier living. Even the trails leading west were little more than paths marked by gravesites. Young Virginia Reed, on her way to California, left her grandmother in a grave under a burr oak in Kansas. Susan Magoffin, bound for New Mexico with her freight-hauling husband, buried her first child near Bent's Fort and the Purgatoire River. Fanny Kelly lost her 5-year-old adopted daughter to Indians while crossing Wyoming. And Frances Grummond had to suffer the loss of her husband while listening to Army carpenters slap together coffins for the other 80 men that died with him.

Some feared the Indians and the misery and destruction they wrought on female travelers. Fanny Kelly's loss of her little daughter would have been difficult enough for most to endure, but in addition, she suffered several months of captivity among the Sioux Indians. On the other hand, Cynthia Ann Parker had no fear of captivity among the Comanches, rather captivity among civilized whites killed her.

Adventure lured some women to the West. Frances Roe accompanied her West Point graduate husband, Lt. Fayette Roe, on his assignment into Colorado, Oklahoma and Montana. She enjoyed hunting and horseback riding. And she shared most of the danger that her infantry husband confronted. Kitty LeRoy, who died in the West, was a dancer. The excitement and adventure she found in the West no doubt contributed to her dying there. She was only in her late 20s when they found her shot to death in a dreary hotel room. And a couple years later, in Cheyenne, on a warm Indian-summer night, a shoot-out in the street in front of Miss Hamilton's House for "Working Girls," left Edmund Malone dead. His girlfriend worked for Miss Hamilton. A quarrel with Ida Snow, induced by elections and encouraged by whiskey, sent Malone to a lonely grave. But he was not alone long. Ida Snow died less than 10 months later of "apoplexy." She was buried beside Malone.

Josephine Earp found adventure in Tombstone, Arizona with the famous Wyatt Earp. She joined Earp shortly after he had arrived in Tombstone and suffered through the killing times that Wyatt, his brothers, and friend, Doc Holliday, brought to that southeast Arizona mining town. With Earp to his dying day, Josephine was happy to trail along throughout the West, even to Alaska before she and the famous gunslinger settled down in Los Angeles.

And then there were the reformers. They came West for a different reason. Actually, in the eyes of some, most of the women that came West were reformers. A Wisconsin newspaper noted in 1846 that "the influence of one virtuous and refined woman will subdue more ferocity than half a dozen male missionaries." Another newspaperman noted, "Whatever may be the customs of a country, the women of it decided the morals."

In the early days of reforming in the West, missionaries went among the Indians trying to convert them to Christianity. Mary Clementine Collins was one of those kind of reformers. She spent several decades among the Indians in the Dakotas teaching and preaching. When the Indians were civilized enough, crusaders sought other outlets for their religious vigor. One of those outlets was the age-old battle against alcoholic beverages. With a hatchet in one hand and the Bible in the other, Carry Amelia Moore Nation, attacked Kansas drinkers, then took her crusade on the road, even visiting countries in Europe.

As to men in the West, they wanted women, any kind of women. One old Texan told a British traveler in 1841, "Wimmen was powerful scarce in these diggins, and almost any sort of one was looked on as a regular *find*."

California miners often claimed that "women were scarcer than gold." Army regulations called for one laundress to 19 and one-half soldiers, but that never satisfied the soldiers. As a result of those shortages, prostitutes also came West. Their lives were perhaps the most unpredictable. A typical prostitute was in her teens. And she retired, usually in her early 20s—unless she died first. The hazards of the trade included venereal disease, abortion, alcoholism, laudanum overdose, or a bullet from a jealous lover's gun—or one from another prostitute whose customers she stole. And they went by some of the more colorful names in the West: Molly b'Damn, Contrary Mary, Squirreltooth Alice, Big Nose Kate, and Louisville Lou.

Colorful names were not restricted to bawdy ladies, however. A gal called "Snapping Annie" was a bullwhacker. And an elderly woman around Cheyenne was called "Apple Annie." She spent her waking hours trying to survive by selling apples door to door in the city's saloons.

Women in the West did what they had to do to survive. One woman, the mother of five, headed up a gang of rustlers that purportedly rustled 500 head of cattle in one raid. Another woman, longing for curtains, made do with "a bale of fringed buckskins" she traded from an Indian for 10 lbs. of sugar.

But life could be harsh too. George Law cut a dug-out shelter out of a small hill and settled his wife and eight children there while he set out to open the first coal mine in the vicinity of Rock Springs, Wyoming.

One bride set up frontier housekeeping with a buffalo robe thrown across a quaker-post bunk, a Dutch oven, a frying pan or two, a dog "and not much of anything else."

Another, on reaching her new home, a dirt-floored, one-room cabin, cleaned it as best she could, washed a stack of filthy dishes, brought towels and linens and a chamber pot "that a bride would need, but that a man would never think of."

One pioneer's wife in northwest Colorado settled in with her husband, three children and a "shirt-tail-full" of cattle and never saw another white woman for three years.

On the other hand, one common-law wife, only the second white woman in her particular area, arrived in the West with her common-law husband, but soon grew tired of him. While he was away, she left the homestead with one of the ranch hands and journeyed to New Mexico. She grew tired of her new mate and within the next year, returned to her former husband. As far as is known, she lived happily ever after.

Sometimes, the problems women faced in the West were full of humor. A widow woman running a cattle ranch in the Colorado Rockies was faced with a particular dilemma one evening that she handled quite well. As this handsome widow puttered around her kitchen, the door suddenly swung open and in rode a drunken cowboy on his favorite horse.

The widow woman said nothing, but calmly turned and walked from the room. While the drunken cowboy sat astride the startled horse wondering what his next move might be, the widow lady returned with a double-barrelled shotgun, the breech open and two shells in her fingers. As she dropped the shells into the chambers, the cowboy made a quick exit.

Outside, horse and cowboy headed for safety, riding into the surrounding prairie. The last thought he had was: "The white-haired woman meant business and he still was within range."

Just as he dived out of the saddle, the shotgun roared. When they found his horse the next morning, the cantle was full of buckshot. Needless to say, the drunken cowboy never bothered the widow again.

And sometimes, Western woman's life was full of tragedy. One hard-working pioneer wife became ill, but managed to get the medication she needed to try to tame the illness. She carefully placed her medication in the cabinet of a clock to keep it from her children. Unknown to her, her husband also kept the arsenic he used to kill coyotes in the same cabinet. One day, by mistake, the woman took the arsenic.

Was the woman of the Old, Wild West a heroine, or a survivor? Was she brave, or merely doing what she had to do? Was she foolhardy in following her husband west, or was she only being true to her man?

Unfortunately, there is a problem with arriving at answers to such questions. Diaries, newspapers and occasional letters have preserved some of the women's stories. But the interview with the homesteader's wife in a sod-fronted dugout while her husband was in Chicago or Minneapolis trying to earn enough to buy seed for spring planting, that interview cannot be. Nor can we walk along with a Sioux mother, searching for a sacred spot to bury her son killed in one of the many soldier raids on an Indian camp. Nor can the wife of an enlisted man killed in the Custer Fight come forward to tell her story.

Therefore, many of their stories are indeed lost. For those that did keep diaries, write letters and even publish books, they afford a brief glimpse at life for Western women.

1

The Parker Saga:
Cynthia and Quanah Parker

This story of the Parkers is a tale of four generations of pioneer Americans. Beginning with John Parker, born in colonial Virginia in time for the Revolutionary War, the story continues through John's son Silas Parker and Silas' brothers. Silas Parker's daughter Cynthia Ann is the next link, and her son Quanah Parker completes the four-generation chain of events.

John Parker's descendents fought their way across the North American continent through almost 150 years of history. And when the land around them became too settled, they moved on. By 1818, when John Parker arrived in Illinois, he had lived in Elbert County, Georgia and Bedford County, Tennessee.

In Illinois, the Parkers settled on the eastern border in Crawford County, then trekked north to Coles County six years later. The families Bates, Doty, Frost and Kellogg soon followed.

By 1833, High Johnny, as John Parker came to be known, now in his 70s, lacked the elbow room that he liked. Again, he gathered his family and friends and set out for new horizons. In the fall of 1833, Parker's collection settled on the Texas frontier.

The group claimed land in the wooded, upper valley of the Navasota River near present Groesback (Limestone County), along a vague line where Post Oak Savannah vegetation gradually fades into the Blackland Prairie. An ideal spot, perhaps the best John Parker had ever settled, the soil was rich with abundant pasturage, excellent water, ample game and good timber.

But the Texas frontier was far from paradise. When American settlers first arrived, they were well treated by the Indian tribes they came into contact with. As settlers encroached more and more, friction between the two cultures developed. The first trouble affecting the Parkers involved Colorado settlers north of the Parker settlement. Those settlers molested a band of Tehuacanas Indians camped in the hills near present Tehuacana, Texas. The pioneers from Colorado tried to steal ponies from the Indians. The Tehuacanas retaliated and two whites died and set all local whites on edge.

Cautiously, the Parkers built a fort during 1834. Fort Parker covered nearly an acre, had two sturdy blockhouses at diagonal corners and tough walls of hewn cedar timbers. There were potholes in the 15-foot walls and the upper story of the blockhouses jutted out over the lower story. The fort completed, the Indian problem stood solved.

But Texas settlers faced a new problem. Mexico had a new leader. He asked burning questions about rule violations by American settlers in Mexico's Texas country. The Mexican dictator, Antonio Lopez de Santa Anna, asked about land grants, duties on imports, and illegal possession of slaves. (Slavery was not permitted in Mexico.)

As the Parkers saw it, these were not their problems. But in 1836 when Santa Anna's army marched north to roust defiant Texans, the Parkers fled their tiny settlement for Fort Houston, 50 to 60 miles east. The flooded Trinity River stopped them short of their destination. It was there on the Trinity in late April or early May that word came that Sam Houston and his army had defeated Santa Anna at San Jacinto. The jubilant Parker group returned to their fort, ready now to get on with spring planting.

Through May 18, men, women and children gathered scattered stock and worked the soil. Seldom had they been happier. It was, however, the events of the next 24 hours that burned a spot in Texas history for the Parkers, and scarred the hearts of participants for life.

The sun rose just after 5 a.m. on May 19, 1836, a Thursday. One of the Fort Parker settlers remembered, "It was no day for the awful deeds committed, for nature had ushered into light a May-day as gentle and as serene as the soft light of the dawning sun that stole carelessly over our sleeping farms."

John Parker's son, James, and James' sons-in-law, L.D. Nixon and Luther T.M. Plummer, were in their fields a mile from the fort before the sun broke over the Navasota River bottoms. Seth Bates, Elisha Anglin, and an old man called Lunn either left Fort Parker early, or slept in rough cabins near their farms. All worked long hours and the walk to the fort each night was tiring and a waste of valuable daylight.

The Faulkenberrys, David and son Evan, and Silas M. and Benjamin F.; Samuel Frost; Mrs. Doty (or Duty); Mrs. Nixon, Sr. (or Nickson); George E. Dwight and their families remained.

One fort inhabitant remembered, "While a few of our more delicate ones were still engaged in slumber, we noticed upon an eminent point on the prairie, not exceeding four hundred yards from the fort, a body of restless Indians." Estimates of the combined Comanche-Kiowa-Caddoan band ranged from 500 to 800.

Sarah Nixon fought panic and slipped out of the fort to try and gather the men working in the fields. Others watched the Indians. Finally, about nine o'clock, a dirty white cloth on a lance conspicuously appeared, indicating peace.

In the fort the nervous inhabitants awaited the Indians next move. The horseman carrying the soiled flag rode with several companions toward the open gates. Within a few hundred feet, the group reined their ponies. The flag-bearer advanced alone.

Benjamin F. Parker, John's bachelor son, stood at the gate, his eyes fixed on the lone rider. Taking slow, deliberate strides, Benjamin walked outside, confronting the rider.

Somewhere a child sobbed softly as Benjamin began a short interview with the dark man on horseback. Reading the sign language, a few in the fort knew that the Indian wanted beef and water. Silas, Benjamin's brother, feared for his brother's life. Suddenly, Benjamin spun on his heel, walked quickly back to the gate, and met the anxious Silas.

To Silas and the others, Benjamin said he thought the Indians intended to fight. Still, he cautioned, he would try to treat with them. Silas pleaded with Benjamin not to return outside the fort. Shaking off the pleas, Benjamin turned and walked away.

The happenings of the next few seconds were punctuated by what witnesses called "wild, infuriated yells" and "hideous warwhoops." Benjamin Parker lay sprawled, a spear through his chest. John Parker springed out the gates, his wife Granny and Elizabeth Kellogg almost dragging behind him.

Mrs. James W. Parker screamed wildly at her children as she fled the fort. Everywhere Comanche and Kiowa ponies skittered, kicking dust, adding to the confusion. Mrs. Nixon, Sr. and Mrs. Doty ran from the fort, as did several others. Silas M. Parker yelled for his wife and four children and found his niece, Rachel Plummer. Rachel, four months pregnant, her 18-month-old son, James Pratt Plummer in her arms, reeled madly through the dust and Indians at the fort entrance. Silas fought to rescue her, but was killed. Rachel fled, escaping into an open field. Minutes later, she was caught by, in her words, "a huge, savage warrior, painted and begrimmed with dust and blood."

Samuel M. and Robert Frost died in the fort. Their effort allowed several women to escape.

From the fort to the wooded river bottom, warriors chased those that had escaped. Nearly a mile away, John Parker, Granny and Mrs. Kellogg were captured. John was stripped, speared and scalped.

Granny, stripped to her underwear, was speared and left for dead. Elizabeth Kellogg escaped death, but was captured.

Meanwhile, Sarah Nixon found the farmers in the field. Luther Plummer and James Parker listened to the breathless girl, planning their action as she spoke. Parker ran unarmed toward the fort. Plummer hurried to the adjoining farms to warn Sarah's husband, L.D. Nixon, and the others.

James Parker soon met his sobbing wife and children, safe from the massacre. In the meantime, Plummer warned Nixon and continued toward the Faulkenberrys and Bateses.

Unarmed, L.D. Nixon trotted only a few hundred yards when he spied Silas Parker's wife Lucy. She carried a baby and led nine-year-old Cynthia Ann, six-year-old John, and a younger child. Suddenly, Lucy Parker stood surrounded by Indians. She and her children were captured.

Nixon continued directly to the fort and was in danger of being killed when David Faulkenberry arrived with a gun. The Indians retreated, permitting Nixon, Lucy Parker, and Lucy's smallest children to escape. John and Cynthia Ann were already lost in the crowd of nearby Indians; Faulkenberry could not help them.

Satisfied that all was lost at the fort, L.D. Nixon left in search of his wife. Before long, he found the George E. Dwight family and those alive from Samuel Frost's. They joined James W. Parker and his family. Sarah Nixon was safe with them. Together, they fled into the Navasota bottoms to hide.

Faulkenberry's gun and Lucy Parker's dog kept a band of Indians at bay long enough for Silas H. Bates, Abram Anglin and Evan Faulkenberry, all armed, to come up and fend off the attackers. Luther Plummer was with them, but unarmed.

Seconds later, the group plodded, almost in a daze, toward safety in the river bottoms. Luther Plummer finally inquired about his wife, realizing for the first time that she was nowhere around. None remembered seeing her. Borrowing a knife, Plummer turned back toward the fort. No one tried to stop him. Within the hour, the others, along with Seth Bates and Mr. Lunn, were safely lost in the tall pecan, post oak and Texas hickory.

The two frightened groups, those with David Faulkenberry and those in the Parker-Dwight-Frost combination were separated. It would be weeks before they knew each others fate.

When night came, Abram Anglin and Evan Faulkenberry visited the fort to search for survivors. Three-fourths of a mile from the fort, the boys found Granny Parker. She begged the young men to find $106.50 in silver buried under a bush at the fort.

Leaving Granny, Abram and Evan slipped into the dark fort. There were no survivors, but they found the silver. Quickly, they returned to the bottoms with the silver and Granny.

Two mornings later, the Faulkenberry group moved east for Fort Houston, three miles from present Palestine in Anderson County.

The Parker-Dwight-Frost group retreated south to Tinnin's at the old San Antonio-Nacogdoches Crossing.

Of the survivors, Granny Parker and Mrs. Doty soon died from their wounds. And if not for the captives taken that day by the combined Comanche-Kiowa-Caddoan band, the story of the Parkers and their friends might have ended.

Not long after the attack on the fort, the Indians left, taking Elizabeth Kellogg, Rachel Plummer and her son, James Pratt Plummer; and Silas Parker's two children, Cynthia Ann and John. Since this was an unusually large raiding party, the bands split the next morning. Elizabeth Kellogg went to the Kichaies, a Caddoan tribe. The Kichaies sold her to a band of Delaware who offered her to Sam Houston. Houston paid the Delaware $150 and six months after her capture, she was free.

Rachel Plummer and her son, James Pratt Plummer, were separated when the tribes divided. In October, Rachel gave birth to a son. Six weeks later, the baby was killed by Rachel's captors. The child interfered with her work as a servant, they claimed. About a year later, she was ransomed by buffalo hunters. They found her 17 days north of Santa Fe in the Rockies. Taken to Independence,

Missouri, she finally returned to the home of James W. Parker, her father, arriving February 19, 1838. Her health and spirit broken, Rachel died exactly one year later without learning the fate of her son James.

In 1842, the Delaware tribe brought the boy to Camp Cooper (later Fort Gibson) and ransomed him. Early in 1843, he came home to his grandfather's, James W. Parker.

Silas M. Parker's two children, six-year-old John and nine-year-old Cynthia Ann, spent much of their lives among the Comanches. John lived with the Comanches until he was stricken with smallpox and left to die in Mexico. Some say he was nursed back to health by a captive Mexican girl, Donna Juanita Espinosa, whom he later married. They lived in Mexico, returning to Texas to search for his sister on one occasion, and later to join the Confederate Army. Most agree that he ran a stock ranch in northern Mexico following the war.

Cynthia Ann Parker remained with the Comanches for 25 years. Her life was a happy one. She married a Kwahadi Comanche, Peta Nokoni, when she came of age. They had three children: Quanah, Pecos and Topsannah. Several attempts to ransom her ended in failure. In one attempt, Col. Leonard Williams' offer of 12 mules and two loads of merchandise was refused. Nor would she talk to Williams. Indian Agent Robert S. Neighbors reported to the U.S. Office of Indian Affairs in 1847 that she could not be coaxed into leaving her adopted people. In 1852, Capt. Randolph B. Marcy heard of a white woman named Parker living with the Indians. Marcy reported to the Secretary of War that he had met John Parker, Cynthia Ann's brother. John told Marcy that she refused to return, explaining that "her husband, children, and all she held most dear, were with the Indians."

During the fall of 1860, a Comanche band raided through Parker County, Texas. Col. Middleton T. Johnson pursued them, failed to catch them and was recalled. Capt. Lawrence Sullivan Ross of the Texas Rangers was ordered out. A sergeant and 20 men of the Second U.S. Cavalry from Camp Cooper joined Ross' Tonkawa scouts. Seventy civilians from Palo Pinto County under Ranger Capt. Jack Cureton rounded out the force.

A few weeks later, on a cloudy December day, Ross' forces found a camp in the rough buttes and canyons on the Pease River near present Crowell, Texas. Nearly 33 years later, in a letter, Ross explained, "I visited neighboring high points to make discoveries. To my surprise I found myself within two hundred yards of a large Comanche village located on a small stream winding around the base of a hill."

Ross added that "a cold piercing wind from the north was blowing, bearing with clouds of dust, and my presence was thus unobserved and the surprise complete."

Down near the river, robed figures moved about, their faces half covered by blankets. Little children huddled together and a few men, mostly slaves, lashed buffalo meat to pack horses. The camp's men and leader, Peta Nokoni, hunted some distance away. Only later would they hear of the raid on their unprotected women and children.

None in the camp looked to the top of the hill; none heard the lunging horses on the steep incline. When the popping guns filtered through the howling wind of the north, the scouts and civilian volunteers were nearly in the camp.

Naduah, or Preloch, as she was sometimes called, was away from the main thrust of the attack. Grabbing her 18-month-old daughter, she mounted a fast pony and broke away. Nearby her husband's Mexican slave, Nokoni's Joe, took his woman behind him on a horse and rode in the same direction.

Capt. Ross and Lt. Kelliher chased Nokoni's Joe and the robed Naduah. In an exchange of arrows and bullets, the girl and Nokoni's Joe were killed by Ross and his servant.

Lt. Thomas Kelliher, in the meantime, rode within pistol range of the fleeing Naduah. Suddenly, the robe blew off Naduah's head. Kelliher, seeing that his prey was a woman with a child, holstered his weapon and stopped her a few yards farther on. Not realizing the

Cynthia Parker and Topsannah, or Prairie Flower, shortly before they both died of "civilization."
(Author's collection)

significance of his capture, Kelliher complained to Rose, "Captain, I ran me horse most to death and captured a damn squaw."

Sometime later, Naduah was recognized as being white. Her blonde hair was greased in Indian fashion, but the blue eyes clearly separated her from the other women. At Camp Cooper Isaac Parker, former Senator in the Congress of the Republic of Texas and then State Legislator, came from his home in Weatherford to question her.

Parker's questions were met with cold, gloomy silence. Finally, dejected, Parker said, "The name of my niece was Cynthia Ann.' "

Parker wrote later, "The moment I mentioned the name she straightened herself in her seat and, patting herself on the breast, said, 'Cynthia Ann, Cynthia Ann.' "

Parker continued, "A ray of recollection sprang up in her mind, that had been obliterated for twenty-five years. her very countenance changed, and a pleasant smile took the place of a sullen gloom."

In 1861, the Texas State Legislature voted her a pension and a league of land. Living primarily in the Van Zandt-Henderson-Anderson counties area of Texas, Cynthia Ann stayed mostly with her brother and legal guardian, Silas M. Parker.

Despite efforts to make her happy, Cynthia Ann was determined to rejoin her husband and sons. On more than one occasion, she attempted to escape. Each time, she was captured and returned. Civilization did not suit her, nor did she have to endure it for long.

During 1864, while Cynthia Ann visited the home of her brother-in-law Rufe O'Quinn, the little, dark-skinned, five-year-old Topsannah died following a siege with fever. Some claim the child died of civilization.

Regardless, the loss of her only link with her happy past, was too much for Cynthia Ann. She mourned the child's death in the Comanche custom by not eating. According to an Indian informant, Cynthia Ann "literally starved herself to death." Cynthia Ann and Topsannah were buried in Fosterville Cemetery near Frankston, four miles from Poyner, Texas near the Henderson-Anderson County line.

Out where the high plains rise in the Panhandle of Texas, young Quanah, Pecos, and their father, Peta Nokoni, knew nothing of the deaths. During 1864, perhaps even before Cynthia Ann and Topsannah died, Peta Nokoni died on a plum hunt. Pecos died soon after, leaving Quanah the only surviving member of Cynthia Ann's family.

By 1867, when many of the chiefs signed the Medicine Lodge Treaty, Quanah was a subchief and prominent warrior in the Kwahadi band of the Comanches. Disgusted with the treaty, Quanah proclaimed, "Tell the white chiefs that the Kwahadis are warriors and will surrender when the blue coats come and whip us." Over the next years, he remained prominent in the final struggle to preserve his people's way of life.

By 1874, the Indians of the Southern Plains were feeling great pressure from both bluecoats and buffalo hunters. In May, Quanah's Kwahadis attempted a gathering of several bands of Indians at the confluence of Elk Creek and the Red River in present Oklahoma. They were there to hear the medicine man Isatai. Isatai convinced Quanah and the others that his medicine was strong enough to carry them safely through any battle.

The first test of Isatai's medicine came at dawn June 27, 1874. The combined tribes struck a buffalo hunters' camp and supply station at the place called Adobe Walls on the North Canadian River in the Texas Panhandle. It took 28 white hunters with buffalo guns to prove Isatai a false prophet and send the angry Comanches reeling.

Seeking revenge, the Comanches struck hard in Texas during the remaining summer months, but the end was near. It was a hard, hot summer on the plains. Streams and waterholes dried up and locusts swept grass and leaves away. Men and horses suffered that summer.

The U.S. Army was ordered out and put considerable pressures on the Comanches and their Kiowa allies. Troopers from Forts Concho and Griffin in Texas, Fort Union in New Mexico Territory, Fort Lyon in Colorado Territory, and Camp Supply in Indian Territory converged on the Staked Plains. The forces were led by Nelson A. Miles, John W. Davidson and William R. Price. Later, Ranald S. Mackenzie and George P. Buell came out leading more soldiers.

By late fall it was obvious that the war was done; the Indians and the old ways were done. In February 1875, Lone Wolf came in with the Kiowa to surrender at Fort Sill. About three months later, on June 2, Cynthia Ann's son, Quanah Parker, and 407 Kwahadis rode stoically into Fort Sill and surrendered.

Quanah counseled his people to follow the white man's way. By 1886, he was Judge of the Court of Indian Offenses. Also successful in business, Quanah leased his tribes' grazing land to whites for a reported $100,000 a year.

In 1890, near Cache, Oklahoma, Quanah's home, "The White House of the Comanches," was built. With two stories and a wing, the house and nearby outbuildings stood inside a neat, white-washed picket fence. Sometimes called the Star House, large painted stars adorned the roofs of the house and each of the outbuildings.

Over the organ in the parlor, Quanah's mother, Cynthia Ann stared down from a life-sized oil painting copied from a daguerreotype made by A.F. Corning in Fort Worth in 1862.

Highly respected and considered the wealthiest Indian in the United States, Quanah was nationally known. With five other chiefs, he rode in President Theodore Roosevelt's inaugural parade in 1905. An admirer of Roosevelt, Quanah even spoke once of entering politics himself.

Though Quanah seemed to have met all his needs, there was one more task to accomplish. Some say that Quanah's first questions when he surrendered at Fort Sill in 1875 was of the welfare and whereabouts of his mother. The questions went unanswered then and in subsequent years. Now, 35 years later, in 1910, Quanah decided to finalize the search for his mother. He knew she was dead, but her burial site was not known.

Quanah's son-in-law, A.C. Birdsong, searched in Texas until he found the site of Cynthia Ann's and Topsannah's burial. On November 29, 1910, Birdsong shipped the remains to Oklahoma.

The bodies, Topsannah cradled in her mother's arms, were viewed by Quanah and re-interred December 10, 1910, in Post Oak Mission Cemetery seven miles northwest of Cache. Less than three months later, Quanah Parker, last of the great Indian chiefs, was dead.

Comanche headman Quanah Parker beside a painting of his mother and sister.
(Author's collection)

In 1950, a 17-foot monument was placed over the grave with the inscription:

> "Resting here until day breaks and darkness disappears
> is Quanah Parker, the last Chief of the Comanches.
> Died Feb. 21, 1911, Age 64 years."

The remains and monument have since been removed to the Fort Sill Military Cemetery.

2

Susan Magoffin
On the Santa Fe Trail

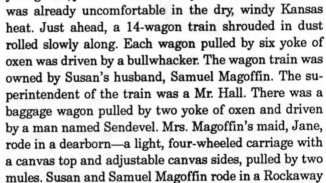

Susan Shelby Magoffin, just over a month shy of her 19th birthdate, was already uncomfortable in the dry, windy Kansas heat. Just ahead, a 14-wagon train shrouded in dust rolled slowly along. Each wagon pulled by six yoke of oxen was driven by a bullwhacker. The wagon train was owned by Susan's husband, Samuel Magoffin. The superintendent of the train was a Mr. Hall. There was a baggage wagon pulled by two yoke of oxen and driven by a man named Sendevel. Mrs. Magoffin's maid, Jane, rode in a dearborn—a light, four-wheeled carriage with a canvas top and adjustable canvas sides, pulled by two mules. Susan and Samuel Magoffin rode in a Rockaway carriage, also pulled by two mules.

Nine and one-half yoke of oxen, two riding horses and three mules were herded along by two men on mules. There were about 20 men. Three were Mexican tent servants for the Magoffins. The total of all animals in the procession was 200 oxen, nine mules, two horses, some chickens and a dog named Ring.

A few days earlier, the Magoffins had arrived in Independence, Missouri, and checked into Smallwood Noland's Hotel. The trade goods they had purchased in the East arrived and were loaded on the wagons. Other preparations were made.

Susan Magoffin, taken in 1945.
(Author's collection)

Early on the morning of June 11, 1846, the Magoffins joined their freight wagons about 10 miles west of Independence at a farm. Susan Magoffin, in a diary entry, wrote, "The cracking of whips, lowing of cattle, braying of mules, whooping and hallowing of the men was a novel sight." It was her entries in that diary that tell the story of her trip to Mexico during 1846 and 1847, the first years of the Mexican War.

Born at the family home, "Arcadia," about six miles south of Danville, Kentucky, on July 30, 1827, Susan was the daughter of Isaac and Marie Boswell Warren Shelby. Her grandfather was Kentucky's first governor. Susan's older sister, Anna, had married Beriah Magoffin, later a Kentucky governor, and on November 25, 1845, at Arcadia, Susan married Beriah's brother, Samuel Magoffin.

That winter, the Magoffins enjoyed a honeymoon trip to the East Coast, living in Philadelphia and New York, but by spring they had decided to haul freight to Santa Fe. At the time, Santa Fe was a Mexican City that traded more with the Americans than with Mexico City far to the south. Susan would join her husband's freight train to Santa Fe and extend their honeymoon. Most claim that Susan was the first white woman to make the trip on the Santa Fe Trail.

Samuel Magoffin's brother, James Wiley Magoffin, had been involved in the Santa Fe trade since 1828. Samuel joined him in 1830.

They had hauled caravans of goods to Mexico and found it profitable. The Magoffins had three trains headed for Santa Fe during this spring of 1846. James had gone ahead with a train, brother William followed with another and Samuel was traveling with this third train that was about 12 days behind William's.

(James Magoffin was on a government mission for U.S. Senator Thomas Hart Benton of Missouri and U.S. President James K. Polk. Magoffin was to prepare the way for the peaceful acquisition of New Mexico by

Samuel Magoffin, taken in 1945.
(Author's collection)

Brigadier General Stephen Watts Kearny. The Mexican War, declared on May 13, 1846, by the U.S. House and Senate, was underway. James Magoffin eventually accompanied soldiers dispatched by Gen. Kearny to treat with the governor of Santa Fe and bring about peaceful occupation of that city.)

Commonly, these freight trains hauled textiles, lead, hardware, cutlery, glassware and similar goods to exchange for Mexican silver, mules, pelts, and blankets.

Missourian William Becknell pioneered freighting along the Santa Fe Trail in 1821. The 800-mile trail ran from Independence, Missouri past Council Grove and westerly until it struck the Arkansas River in present Barton County, Kansas. It hugged the north branch of the Arkansas to Bent's Fort. There, they forded the river and trailed off in a southerly direction to the Raton Pass and through to San Miguel, then along a cutback to the northwest about

40 miles to the 17th century Spanish city of Santa Fe. By 1846, nearly $1,000,000 in trade moved annually over the Santa Fe Trail.

The trip was normally made with oxen since they cost only one-fifth the price of mules. Usually these oxen were steers— range cattle that often weighed 1,000 pounds or more. If a train used mules, then the amount of cargo carried on the wagons was reduced, since grain had to be hauled to feed the mules. Oxen lived on grass along the way. In addition, Indians were not as likely to run off oxen, and if the food supply for bullwhackers was short, they could always kill the oxen for beef. About the only advantage to mules, according to most, was that they traveled faster. The trip to Santa Fe took a week or two less with mules.

The bullwhackers cracked their five-pound whips and cursed the oxen, corralling the Magoffin wagons the first night on the trail at a place called "The Lone Elm," about 35 miles from Independence. (Susan was not pleased. "It is disagreeable to hear so much swearing; I scarcely think they need be so profane.")

That evening, Susan again took up the pen and described her tent: "It is a conical shape, with an iron pole. A cedar table in it is fastened to the pole." Her bed was "as good as many houses have." In their tent, they had carpeting and portable stoves. For supper that night, they ate fried ham and eggs, with biscuits.

Over the next two and one-half months, the Magoffins would dine on "broiled chicken, soup, rice, and a dessert of wine and gooseberry tart; two roasted ducks and baked beans; roast hare and wine; and turkey, prairie chicken, hares and bear." Near Santa Fe, they ate "tortillas made of blue corn"; cheese; two jugs of meat, green peppers and onions boiled together; roasted corn and a fried egg.

Customarily, about six in the morning, the wagonmaster yelled out, "Stretch out!" or "Roll on!" and the train began stretching and rolling over the plains. Not long after, the train would be halted to permit the oxen to urinate. About 10 o'clock, most trains stopped for nooning. While the oxen grazed, the men ate a big breakfast. The train then traveled from one o'clock to five o'clock before stopping for the second and last meal of the day. Following the meal, if there was light left, the train might travel for another mile. For a campsite, they preferred high ground and plenty of grass and water. Early the next morning, one of the men walked through the wagons rapping the iron tires on the wagons to wake everyone and start the new day.

On Sunday, June 14, Susan noted in her diary that the men were not swearing as much. She marveled at the "solemn stillness of a Sabbath on the Prairies." Later, she noted, "The Sabbath on the Plains is not altogether without reverence. Everything is perfectly calm. The blustering, swearing teamsters remembering the duty they owe to their Maker, have thrown aside their abusive language, and are singing the hymns." There was ample time, she pointed out, "for thinking on the great wisdom of our Creator."

By June 16, the train was nearly 100 miles from Independence and Susan wrote, "Oh, this is a life I would not exchange for a good deal! I breathe free without that oppression and uneasiness felt in the gossiping circles of a settled home."

At Council Grove, the train stopped for a few days and prepared their firearms for the Indian troubles they anticipated farther west. On June 21, they made what they called "start number two." Over the next days there was no Indian trouble, but Susan complained about the plight of the oxen. She noted, "They came off with bloody necks from the yoke's rubbing, and their heads and backs well whip-lashed." But she admitted, "Snakes and musquitoes are the only disagreeable parts of my prairie life."

Of mosquitoes she wrote: "It was slap, slap, all the time, from one party of the combatants, while the others came with a buz and a bite." And the mosquitoes bothered the carriage mules causing them to switch "their tails from side to side." It was hot, but she covered herself with a shawl. She told her diary: "Millions upon millions were swarming around me, and their knocking against the carriage *reminded me of a hard rain.*" The next morning, she noted, "I found my forehead, arms and feet covered with knots ... some of them quite as large as a pea."

On July 27, the train arrived at Bent's Fort, where the Purgatoire River met the Arkansas in southeastern Colorado. Six-foot thick adobe walls enclosed "some twenty-five rooms," and there in one of those rooms Susan celebrated her 19th birthday on Thursday, July 30. But she was ill and complained: "The shoeing of horses, neighing, and braying of mules, the crying of children, the scolding and fighting of men, are all enough to turn my head."

Gen. Kearny and 1,700 soldiers from Fort Leavenworth were at the fort preparing to march on to Santa Fe. There were Indians at the fort, too. It was not a good place for a sick person. And Susan

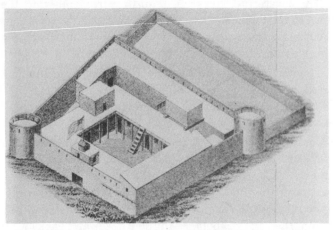

Bent's Fort as it appeared when the Magoffin's were there.
(From Abert's Journal from Bent's Fort to St. Louis in 1845.)

Magoffin felt awful. She wrote, "I am sick! strange sensations in my head, my back, and hips."

The next morning, her pains became more severe and about midnight, she aborted a fetus. It was August 5 before she could get out of bed. After her ordeal, she marveled at an Indian woman who gave birth. The Indian mother gave birth *"and in half an hour after she went to the River and bathed herself and it."*

The fort quieted after Kearny's army left, and on August 7, Magoffin's wagon train, with Susan in the Rockaway carriage, rolled away from Bent's Fort. Crossing the Arkansas River, considered the boundary between Mexico and the United States, was sad for Susan. She was leaving the United States, and with her recent illness, she wrote, "Perhaps I have left it (United States) for not only the first, but the last time."

The days that followed were often long and hard, but by late August, the train began entering the tiny Mexican settlements near Santa Fe. Susan was an attraction to the people of these communities. Many had never seen a white woman. She noted that in one community, children "from the infant in the arm up," gathered "so thick it was hard for any one to pass; none were wholly clad, and some of the little ones in a perfect state of nudity; eyes were opened to their fullest extent, mouths gaped, tongues clattered, and I could only bite my lips and almost swallow my tongue to restrain my laughter."

A little later, however, Susan became embarrassed because the Mexican women wore clothing that left their arms, necks and ankles bare. And when the Mexican women waded in water, they pulled their skirts above their knees!

Finally, on August 30, 1846, Susan Magoffin became "the first American lady" to enter Santa Fe, with the city under the American flag. General Stephen Watts Kearny had occupied Santa Fe without a fight 12 days earlier. Susan and Samuel moved into a four-room house near the church. The walls were whitewashed and covered with calico up to about six feet to protect against people leaning against the whitewash. The floor was dirt. Their first supper was with Samuel's brother, James. They dined on oysters and champagne.

Susan wrote, "The air is fine and healthy; indeed the only redeeming quality of this part of New Mexico is its perfectly pure atmosphere, not the damp unhealthy dews of the States."

Suddenly now, the adventure was not just the successful conquering of the Santa Fe Trail, but she found herself in the middle of the

Mexican War. Before the train's arrival in Santa Fe, word had reached the group that the Mexican governor of New Mexico, Manuel Armijo, had fled rather than fight Kearny's army.

U.S. President James K. Polk had ordered Gen. Zachary Taylor and his command into a disputed area of Texas between the Nueces and Rio Grande Rivers. Mexico considered this an act of war, but the Mexican congress was not in session and it could not make a formal declaration. In May, Pres. Polk wrote a message asking the U.S. Congress for a declaration of war due to the failure of a diplomatic mission to Mexico. Before he could deliver the message, however, word came from Taylor: "Hostilities may now be considered as commenced." Polk altered the speech and asked that Congress acknowledge that a state of war existed "by the act of Mexico herself." By votes of 40-2 in the Senate, and 174-14 in the House, Polk got his declaration of war. Polk claimed Mexico had invaded Texas. Congress appropriated $10 million and called for 50,000 volunteers.

By August, besides Kearny occupying Santa Fe, Taylor had won battles at Palo Alto, Resaca de la Palma and Monterey. And the Americans busied themselves preparing a defense of Santa Fe just in case Gov. Armijo should mount a counterattack.

Fort Marcy, named for Secretary of War William L. Marcy, was built above the city and stood only 600 yards from the heart of Santa Fe. Susan rode with Gen. Kearny to the fort for a visit and wrote, "It is the most perfect view I ever saw. The Fort occupies some two acres of ground, has a double wall built of adobes, the space between being filled with stones and mortar."

The Magoffins left Santa Fe on October 5, headed south with their freight wagons, perhaps to help supply the United States soldiers. Rumors flooded Susan's diary. She heard that Commodore Robert Field Stockton had taken "Calafornia" and that General John Ellis Wool had taken Chihuahua.

Susan noted her first anniversary on November 25 and wrote, "It has been a happy one too."

In December, a rumor had Samuel's brother, James, on trial for spying. And there were other problems. On December 29, Susan wrote: "The Indians are all around us; coming into the soldier's camp and driving off their stock, and killing the men in attendance on them. The enemy are advancing on us as we hear today and have even had a battle with our troops only about eighty miles from us."

Sometimes they stayed in towns along the way; at other times they were traveling and camping. As 1847 dawned, they were still moving and Susan and others were still suffering bouts of illness, mainly "fever." Rebellious outbreaks at San Miguel and at Taos worried Susan. She feared that the Mexican people in the towns might try something and noted that the Magoffins kept handy "a double-barreled shot gun, a pair of holster and one pair of belt pistols, with one of Colts six barreled revolvers."

Through January and into February, 1847, life was hard for Susan. Their wagons continued south, arriving at Dona Ana near present Las Cruces, New Mexico on February 10. She was in El Paso not long after. A February 26 rumor swept their party, claiming that Gen. Zachary Taylor's army was defeated and captured at San Luis Potosi. Two days later, Susan wrote: "I attended mass with the family, not for a show, but to worship God."

There was more bad news and Susan feared that Mexicans in El Paso might rise up against the Americans. Over the next days and weeks, however, Susan and the others found that the war was not going as badly as the rumors announced.

The Magoffins rolled out of El Paso on March 14 and headed downriver to Socorro. By April 4, they had traveled over 200 miles south to the city of Chihuahua where they linked up with Colonel A.W. Doniphan's Missouri volunteers.

The freight wagons followed Doniphan south to Saltillo where, on June 20, word came that a Mexican army of 14,000 was advancing on the city. Susan wrote: "I've heard of wars and rumours of wars and have been as I thought almost in them, but this is nearer than ever." She added, "I've thrown a few things into my trunk in case of retreat." The next day she told her diary: "The attack didn't come."

The Magoffins spent the remainder of June and July in Saltillo and on August 1, 1847 announced to her diary that she was again pregnant. She wrote that "she has a hard time of it, some sickness all the time, heart-burn, head-ache, cramp etc."

In mid-August, a letter from Monterey brought hope that brother James was unharmed, and on August 21, the Magoffins traveled with General Caleb Cushing's soldiers toward Monterey. Susan made the two-day trip in a carriage—"the roughest ride I ever had."

On August 25, Gen. Zachary Taylor visited with her, and she rode out to his camp on the Matamoras road the following day. The camp was in a "thick grove of trees." She recorded, "The general was dressed in his famed old gray sack coat, striped cotton trowsers (sic) blue calico neck-kerchief." She added, "I find him polite, affable and altogether agreeable."

Over the next couple of weeks, Susan and Samuel prepared to return to the United States. The war in Mexico was all but done. General Winfield Scott won victories at Churubusco, Chapultepec and finally, Mexico City, on September 14, 1847. (The treaty ending the war was signed at Guadalupe Hidalgo on February 2, 1848. Ratification took until May 30, and the last American soldiers left Mexico about mid-June, 1848.)

Susan was still not well, her pregnancy being only part of the problem. She was down with yellow fever in Matamoras, Mexico when she gave birth to a child that died not long after.

In the years that followed, the Magoffins suffered much tragedy in their family. They arrived back in the United States late in 1847 and Samuel took Susan to Kentucky where he bought a large estate near Lexington. She bore a son there named James. The child died soon afterwards. A daughter born in 1851, Jane Magoffin, later the wife of George Taylor of Ohio, survived and was responsible for preserving her mother's diary.

In the spring of 1852, the Magoffins moved to St. Louis County, Missouri and built a home at Barrett's Station, a short distance from Kirkwood, Missouri. There, Samuel became involved in farming and real estate. It was there that Susan gave birth to another daughter, Susan.

And it was there in Missouri, on October 26, 1855, that 28-year-old Susan Shelby Magoffin died. The funeral was held at the Pine Street Presbyterian Church in St. Louis, and she was buried in Bellefontaine Cemetery.

Susan's husband, Samuel Magoffin, died on April 23, 1888.

3

Snowkill:
The Donner-Reed Tragedy

The ragged line of ox-drawn wagons creaked lazily out of a dust cloud down the worn track to the adobe-walled fortress. The men and women trudging along beside the wagons stepped more lively now, but the weary oxen with patient power plodded at the same pace, making no move to keep up. They had dragged these prairie schooners over 650 miles from Independence, Missouri. It was nearly all uphill from the Missouri River bottom to this place in Wyoming with an elevation of 4,500 feet. The big Durham oxen had traced that thin strip of water pioneers called a river—the Platte—and hauled their masters to this oasis in the vast wilderness, this place the American Fur Company called Fort Laramie.

Like the men, the women did their share as the wagons rolled west. They did what chores were necessary. Sometimes, they walked beside the wagons; sometimes, they rode. Most of the time they fought the weather and the dust.

Fort Laramie, the trading fort, lay over 500 miles west of the nearest United States soldiers. By day, Cheyenne, Sioux and other bands of natives dotted the plain to the rear of the fort; by night, they chanted their songs into the wee hours of morning. Everywhere Indian dogs barked and ran nipping at the heels of laughing youngsters. Inside the high adobe walls, the fathers and older brothers of the Indian children moved casually, sometimes making a nuisance of themselves, at other times dealing with this curious white man that had joined them in their land.

The weary travelers from Independence wiped the dust from their eyes and the fear from their faces and smiled at the fort, this first sign of civilization in over 600 miles. And it was only the beginning of the trip for over 2,000 pioneers who traveled the Oregon Trail in 1846 America.

The 1830s and early 1840s were depression years in the Mississippi Valley. Many in the valley considered moving west for a new start, a new beginning in a new land. In the wagon train approaching Fort Laramie, the Illinois families of George and Jacob Donner and James Frazier Reed had left their Sangamon County holdings in search of more prosperous times in California.

Earlier, during the spring of 1846, in the Springfield, Illinois *Sangamon Journal* a simple ad appeared: "Who wants to go to California without costing them anything? Need 8 young men. Signed: G. Donner and Others."

George Donner and "Others" included his wife Tamsen and their children, plus his brother Jacob and his family and their good friend, James Reed and family.

The Donners lived on German Prairie, just east of present Springfield, Illinois, "about two miles south of Camp Butler," at the southwest quarter of Section 20, Clear Lake Township 16 North, Range 4.

The Donners were adventurous sorts. The brothers were in their 60s (George 62; Jacob 65) and were considered prosperous. George tried Texas in 1838, but returned the next year and now yearned for California. The Donner brothers were born in North Carolina and arrived in Illinois just prior to the 1830s.

Hard workers, they built small fortunes. Now as they prepared to leave for California, every convenience was accounted for. George Donner's family traveled in three wagons with twelve yoke of oxen.

*The interior of a covered wagon, typical of many of those
that went West in the 19th Century.
(Author's Collection)*

They had five saddle horses and a small herd of beef and milk cattle.
For money, George's wife Tamsen carefully stitched $10,000 in bank
notes into a quilt. Several hired hands accompanied the Donners.
Jacob matched his brother's wagons with equipment.

Their friend James Reed was similarly outfitted. But Reed's
teamsters also drove eight Durham oxen pulling what some have
called a "pioneer palace car." A spectacular vehicle, heavy foot-wide
boards over the wheels made a base for a second story bedroom.
High-backed spring seats awaited the passengers and when the
weather was cool, a little sheet-iron stove was in the center, complete with a stovepipe out the canvas top. Everywhere there were
neat, well-built storage compartments. It housed a library and opposite the side entrance to this pioneer extravaganza was a mirror.

Reed, born in Ireland, came to Galena, Illinois, to work in the
lead mines not long after arriving in the United States. Moving to
the Springfield area in 1831, he quickly succeeded as a farmer, mer-
chant and finally, furniture manufacturer. A town sprung up around
his factory and soon became known as Jamestown, after Reed.

Some called it "Jimtown." Today, the town is the thriving community of Riverton, just off I-72 east of Springfield.

To prepare for the trip, Reed had asked and received, on April 14, 1846, documents from Illinois Governor Thomas Ford and U.S. Representative Edward Dickinson Baker, proclaiming him an upstanding citizen and businessman. In addition, he had appealed to U.S. Representative (and soon-to-be U.S. Senator) Stephen A. Douglas and U.S. Secretary of War William L. Marcy for help in securing an appointment as "Sub-Indian Agent" west of the Rocky Mountains. And he indicated an interest in visiting the Sandwich (Hawaiian) Islands and Oregon before settling in San Francisco.

With the Donners, James Reed and his family gathered in the square at Springfield to begin their trip. It was an event witnessed by many. Even Mary Todd Lincoln and son walked to capitol square to view the wagons and see these daring pioneers off on their adventure. Mrs. Lincoln's husband, Abraham, was away attending to circuit court business, and she made the necessary apologies to Reed. That night, they hawed and geed their teams and wagons to a wooded hill southwest of the State Capitol building and camped on what would, some 20 years later, be graded down for the site of the present Illinois State Capitol building.

On Tuesday, April 14, 1846, just over 30 men, women and children left Springfield, traveling the old Jacksonville Road to begin the three-week trek to Independence, Missouri. At Independence, the jumping-off point for pioneers, the Donner-Reed party joined a larger train and, convinced the grass was tall enough, the season dry enough, and their train large enough, they plunged off into the unknown lands. That was May 12, 1846.

A few days later, the Big Blue River near present Manhattan, Kansas, stopped them. The river was flooded. They were forced into camp to build boats and rafts for crossing. It was in that camp that the adventure had its first casualty when Sarah Keyes, James Reed's sickly mother-in-law, died. It was the last of May and Virginia Reed, Mrs. Keyes' granddaughter, wrote a letter to a cousin in

Edwardsville, Illinois: "We made a nete coffin and buried her under a tree...."

They cut the coffin from a cottonwood tree. They split the wood and hewed and planed it. Mrs. Keyes was buried under a burr oak with the soft sobs of her family and the quiet words of a Cumberland Presbyterian minister helping her on her way. Someone carved the particulars into the tree:

"Sarah Keyes, aged 70 years. Died 29th May, 1846.
From Springfield, Illinois."

Finally across the Big Blue, the wagon train aimed in a northwesterly direction. For the 300 travelers monotony soon set in, disrupted only by occasional bands of hungry Indians wanting little more than food and cattle from the travelers. And every night was like the last. Guards were posted to protect the cattle. Others gathered wood and water for cooking. They ate bacon, coffee, bread and flap-jacks too often, then with a full stomach bedded down.

Day after day they traced the broad ribbon of shallow, sluggish water called the Platte. The wagons were drawn by Grand Island and Fort Childs (later Fort Kearny). The pioneers watched Court-house Rock (named for the Old Courthouse in St. Louis), Jail Rock, Chimney Rock, and Scotts Bluff slip by. The sun rose in the east and day after day the wagons moved west with it. And then, they neared Fort Laramie.

The land was even more barren now and the thorny cactus aggravated animals and men, too easily punching holes in worn boots and shoes. Just east of the fort, they met James Clyman. Clyman, a trapper and mountain man, was from Illinois. Clyman had been in the same Black Hawk War company (Captain Jacob M. Early's Mounted Volunteers) as Abraham Lincoln and James Reed. The members of the train inquired about the route west. There was talk, especially in the Donner-Reed party, about not following the traditional route to Fort Hall, but cutting off at Fort Bridger to the southwest, around the Great Salt Lake and across the mountains to the Bay of San Francisco. The Hastings Cutoff, they called it.

Clyman cocked his head and smiled wryly, "It is barely possible to get through if you follow it and may be impossible if you don't. Take the regular wagon track, and never leave it," Clyman warned his friends. Even on horseback it was a bad time. He told Reed and the others he had just ridden through there after being in California since 1844. He knew about such things, had been a surveyor, and reminded them they were already behind schedule. Over two months they had traveled and still were only a third of the way to California. Clyman shook his head at any discussion of the cutoff and sternly reminded Reed and the others of the "roughness of the Sierras."

That was enough for most. They would stick with the traditional route, go by way of Fort Hall. But somehow the Donners and James Reed still considered the Hastings route! They had their heads set on it.

Reed and the Donners dug out their copy of *The Emigrants Guide to Oregon and California* by Lansford W. Hastings and read from it again and again. The book, published in Cincinnati in 1845, proclaimed: "The most direct route for the California emigrants, would be to leave the Oregon route, about two hundred miles east from Fort Hall; thence bearing west southwest, to the Salt Lake; and thence continuing down to the bay of St. Francisco."

Following a short rest at Fort Laramie, the big train stretched out across Wyoming toward present Casper. The canvas-covered wagons rolled over the barren land of blue-gray sage to the Sweetwater River and Independence Rock, then trailed southwest through South Pass. Oxen, wagons and people forded the murky Green River and ground out the final thirty miles to Fort Bridger.

It was late in July when the parade of more than 70 wagons filed up to the fort built three years earlier by "Old Gabe," as Jim Bridger was called. The fort claimed a collection of big log buildings and a horse pen. There was plenty of grass, water and timber. Talk was of this new Hastings Cutoff. Bridger had nothing but good to say about it. There is no evidence that the Donners and Reeds met with Bridger or his partners, but he was eager to get trains moving along the cutoff. He thought those using the cutoff were making a smart move.

What Bridger did not tell them was that for nearly two years, travelers had been using the Sublette Cutoff to get to Fort Hall, bypassing Bridger's fort. His trading business was hurting.

Yes, indeed, Bridger recommended the Hastings route. A 60-wagon Harlan-Young party had just pulled out a short time before along the same path, the *shortcut* to California. Some claim Bridger's partner Louis Vasquez even had a letter that warned against a part of the Hastings' route. But Vasquez, like Bridger, had nothing to gain by discouraging trains from coming by their fort.

And if Bridger had a motive, so did Hastings. Lansford W. Hastings wanted settlers in California. More Americans meant a better chance for government in California, thus providing Hastings with a political base so that he could become Governor, or President, or King, or whatever. So Hastings' guidebook made the trip sound like a Sunday afternoon stroll.

The decision was made. They would travel the cutoff!

This train elected a new leader, George Donner, and with 20 wagons and 74 people, they headed west southwest from Fort Bridger on July 31, 1846.

Three wagons and 13 extra people, all bent on traveling to California the *short* way, joined them just a few days later. But then as they prepared to enter Weber Canyon and work their way down to the valley of the Great Salt Lake, they found a note left for them. Hastings himself, traveling with the Harlan-Young party, had left word that the canyon was blocked. He urged someone to ride ahead and contact him. Then Hastings would explain an easier route. Reed, aboard his gray racing mare named Glaucus, rode ahead for the information.

The new route was through the Wasatch Mountains. But a storm had blocked the route there too and they inched their way along

13-year-old Virginia Reed,
shown here some years later, survived
the Donner-Reed tragedy.
(Author's Collection)

clearing the boulder-strewn, canyon-cut path. They fought miles of tangled scrub forest. It was no place for green pioneers. Their tempers shortened; they longed for the milder hardships of the gentle plains between Missouri and Fort Laramie. It took them nearly a month to travel 50 miles. It was too much for one of the travelers. Luke Halloran was his name. He died near the Great Salt Lake. Consumption killed him. He was in his mid-twenties.

Finally at the oasis at the east edge of the Great Salt Lake, they reckoned the desert would not be so harsh. It was flat, but nothing like the long, grueling struggle through the rugged Wasatch. And besides, Hastings promised the desert could be crossed in two days.

It took over five days! The desert was 80 miles of glaring salt and sand. The lack of water and the blazing heat sapped the Durham oxen. Reed watched horrified as the great beasts bawled for water. To save them, he sent two of his hired men to try and find water. Sometime that night, the oxen strayed and were lost.

Indians in the desert, known as Diggers, harassed the weary travelers. And they waited. They waited for cattle to give out. They waited for the white men to improve their miserable desert menu of roots, carcasses and large crickets.

Little Virginia Reed, in a letter to her Springfield cousin the next year, wrote of this time, "Thay pursuaded us to take Hastings cutof over the salt plain thay said it saved 3 Hundred miles. we went that road & we had to go through a long drive of 40 miles With out water Hastings said it was 40 but i think 80 miles."

Continuing, Virginia wrote of one night in the desert: "We laid down on the ground we spred one shawl down we laid down on it and spred another over us and then put the dogs on top it was the couldes night you most ever saw the wind blew and if it haden bin for the dogs we would have Frosen."

Finally, Charles Stanton and William McCutchen were sent ahead to California and Sutter's, a fortified post built by John Sutter at the site of present Sacramento, California in 1839. They were to fetch supplies to replenish what had been lost. They rode out just after the middle of September and when the desert was nearly behind them.

And it was a good thing for when the Donner party came out of the desert and rested at the spring near Pilot Peak, they counted their lost oxen and cattle at 100. In addition, several wagons were abandoned, including Reed's palace car.

At the Pilot Peak spring, they regrouped and prepared for the next leg of the journey. The trail would lead them southwest, then north to Mary's River (presently the Humboldt River). Not far from Pilot's Peak, the pioneers decided to split their train to allow for more grass for the oxen and cattle. The Donners took the lead group; Reed took the other. They reached Mary's River the last day of September and began winding their way west.

The frustrating journey continued wearing on the minds and hearts of the weary travelers. The going was tough; the terrain demanding. On October 5th, the teams were working hard to get up a hill. Some had doubled their ox teams to drag the wagons over the crest, but one young teamster, John Snyder, tried to make it with his regular team. Milford ("Milt") Elliot, Reed's teamster, superintendent of livestock, and right-hand man, attempted to guide his oxen and wagon around Snyder's team. Elliot's whip, some say, inadvertently struck Snyder's oxen causing them to bolt and become tangled with those Elliot drove.

An enraged Snyder, according to one story, began thrashing the oxen with his whip. Reed, incensed that anyone would treat the precious oxen so, intervened and was struck with the butt of Snyder's whip. A long gash opened on Reed's head and blood flowed over his face. Mrs. Reed ran to help her husband. She was struck down by the muscular Snyder, and Reed, in the confusion, slashed at Snyder with his knife, driving it home below the collarbone and into young Snyder's lung. Still on his feet, Snyder struck both Reed and his wife again. Snyder's last blow knocked James Reed to his knees and opened up another cut on his head.

Snyder dropped the whip and turned up the hill, his steps unsure and staggering. Little Billy Graves went to him and was there as Snyder fell.

Virginia and the Reed girls went to their father, but as he saw Snyder collapse, he rushed to him. He still held the bloody knife in his hand and before he got to Snyder, he flung it into the Humboldt River. He kneeled beside Snyder. Some recalled that Snyder spoke, telling him, "I am to blame." Others claimed they did not hear that.

Snyder was teamster for the Graves family. He was also courting (or engaged to) their 20-year-old daughter, Mary Ann. The Graveses witnessed the incident and their sympathies led them to insist on Reed's life in exchange for Snyder's.

Reed was not popular in the section of the train he led. Some blamed him for leading them on this hazardous trail instead of by way of the Fort Hall route. The criticism had been steady since the difficulty working their way down through the Wasatch Mountains. Now only Reed's family, William Eddy, Milt Elliot and John Denton stood up for Reed. The Donners, Reed's Springfield friends, were far ahead and knew nothing of the incident until later. Elliot, Eddy and Denton persisted in defending their friend and finally, the Graveses yielded and permitted Reed his life, a horse and banishment from the company.

The next morning, Reed, his head bandaged, helped bury Snyder. They wrapped the body in a shroud, dug a grave, placed a board on the bottom and one over the top of the body and threw the dirt in on it all.

Reed rode ahead to the Donners, was joined by Walter Herron, a teamster with the Donners, and proceeded toward California to seek help for the entire group. Reed carried a letter to Sutter promising to pay for emergency supplies and services. Just over the mountains, they met Charles Stanton leading pack mules. Reed and Herron continued to Sutter's. Stanton led the mules on east across the mountains. (Reed and Herron's trek was not without drama as they ran short of food. On one occasion, while nearly starved, they found and shared five beans. A walnut-sized piece of rancid tallow was a meal on another occasion.)

Back in the Donner party, the treacherous trail continued reaping its harvest. An aged Belgian cutler named Hardkoop fell behind and was abandoned not long after Reed left. An old German named Wolfinger was also lost. Some said the Indians got him. (A young German, Joseph Reinhardt, later admitted the murder of Wolfinger, with Spitzer's help.) Later on a young man was accidently shot and killed. And from time to time, there was the threat of Indians.

Still the group continued on, hoping against hope to make the mountains before the snow drifted and blocked the narrow passages that could lead them to life in the sunshine of California. But hard luck continued to plague all of them. Animals died or were lost. Guns broke and so did wagons. Young Virginia Reed's pony, Billy, was lost. Their shoes wore out. And then they were down to their last food.

The lead wagons made Truckee Meadows on October 18.

Others pulled in a couple of days later. While they rested at Truckee Meadows, Charles Stanton arrived from Sutter's in California. He brought seven pack mules with flour and dried beef and two guides, Luis and Salvadore. William McCutchen was sick and stayed behind. And, yes, James Reed made it to Sutter's. He was organizing a rescue party. No need to worry about snow. Most said snow was a month away. Stanton inflated their spirits.

But the skies were lead-gray. With the oxen fed well on tall, lush grass in the meadow and abundant water from the Truckee River, the remaining wagons began the 7,000-foot ascent toward the granite mountain that stood between the travelers and the Sacramento Valley and safety. It was a bad mountain even in fair weather and already the peaks were snowcapped. It was too steep. Some remembered John Clyman's warning, how he said that even on horseback, this was a cruel way to go to California.

When they had trudged up to the elevation of Truckee Lake (later Donner Lake), their hopes were still high. Sixty of the group made it to the lake and began considering the trip across the pass. Already the nights were uncomfortably cool. Some predicted snowfall could not be far off.

Three families eager to cross despite their weariness attacked the mountain almost immediately. They were stopped and turned back by five-foot, shoulder-deep drifts. The snows had arrived!

Adamant, another attempt was made on November 3. Again the snow-clogged barrier was too much. This group was caught in a storm and lost their cattle. They wheeled and fled back to the lake and ramshackle cabins that existed. These cabins were built in 1844 by the Murphy-Shallenberger party. And with bits and pieces of their belongings they had saved from the ravages of the murderous trek from Fort Bridger, they constructed more crude huts. Then the snows whipped down onto the Truckee Lake camp. The optimism was blasted out of them by the harshness of nature.

Farther down, about five or six miles from those that made it to the lake, George and Jacob Donner and their families and hired hands (21 in all) remained on Alder (later Donner) Creek, trapped by a snowstorm. Their luck was no better. George Donner's wagon broke an axle and as he shaped another with cutting tools, he sliced his hand and the cut became infected.

And more snow fell. It became harder to keep track of the cattle. Some died and were lost under 20-foot-deep drifts. They struggled to keep holes dug in the drifts so that they could continue to get in and out of their rude, canvas and ox-hide roofed huts.

Some hunted for food, but most animals made their way down the mountain. William Eddy killed a coyote, an owl, two ducks and a squirrel. The grizzly bear he shot was greasy, but welcome. At this elevation, animals could not survive. The snow stacked to 60 feet high in some places before the winter was done.

Young Baylis Williams, none too healthy from the start, died not of starvation, but of malnutrition early in December. Jacob Donner died the same month. Some predicted they were all doomed unless help came soon. Others recalled that God helps those who help themselves.

Charles Stanton had made the trip before. He reckoned as how he could go for help. William Eddy and 15 others wanted to go along. They were, altogether, 10 men, five young women and two boys. Stanton's Indian guides and the others slipped into snowshoes, gathered rations of two mouthsful per day for six days, and walked out of the starving, death-ridden camp, headed for the mountain. It was December 15.

Stanton was the first victim. They abandoned him on the morning of the sixth day. By Christmas day, the others were through the pass on their way down. But only 11 lived and they were starving. There was no food, except...perhaps one of them should be sacrificed to save the others. Better one than all.

But how? Someone suggested that two of them have a shoot-out. Finally, they were coldly reminded that if they wanted someone dead, wait until morning. Surely before the next day dawned, at least one among them would die naturally.

With that sobering thought, they settled into a shivering huddle and waited for the morning to bring an end to the blizzard that mounded snow over them.

The next morning strips of flesh from Patrick Dolan's arms and legs were roasted and eaten. Additional flesh was taken to be dried and eaten later as they moved down toward the Sacramento Valley.

What occurred from then until the group staggered into an Indian village is mostly speculation. Eddy claimed later that he ate only grass. Others said William Foster and the five women ate the two Indian guides.

The five women, Eddy and Foster eventually found the Indian village. They were crawling by then and so pitiful that the impoverished band of Indians could only weep at their appearance.

After a five-day rest and a diet of acorn meal, William Eddy was able to make his way to a nearby ranch, the Johnson Ranch. During the remainder of January preparations were made to rescue those across the pass at the camp near Donner Lake.

At the lake, matters had grown worse. Five at the huts were dead by Christmas. The others survived on field mice, oxhides and tree bark. James Reed's wife Margaret, however, served her four children a Christmas feast. They had ox tripe, a cup of white beans, a few dried apples, a half cup of rice and a tiny square of bacon. Their mother had saved the food for eight weeks.

But the air of optimism James Reed's wife kept up for her children grew dimmer and dimmer. Just after New Year's Day, she and her daughter, Virginia, along with Eliza Williams and Milt Elliot tried to go over the pass. They failed and were driven back to their meek existence. The trip had cost them hope and given them frost-bitten feet.

Mrs. Reed contented herself with keeping the children alive on mice and eventually the family dog, Cash. Twelve-year-old Virginia Reed wrote later that they "had to kill littel cash the dog & eat him we ate his entrails and feet & hide & evry thing about him."

Continuing in this May 16, 1847 letter to her Springfield cousin, Mary C. Keyes, Virginia wrote, "o my Dear Cousin you dont now what trubel is yet. We lived on little cash a week and after Mr. Breen would cook his meat we would take the bones and boil them 3 or 4 days at a time."

These last seven weeks before help arrived, the Reeds subsisted mainly on the roof of their hut—boiled oxhide.

Virginia Reed's mother and father, Mr. and Mrs. James Reed.
(Author's Collection)

William Eddy's arrival in California prompted a swift organization of men and resources to make the trip in spite of the weather, which all knew should be mellowing some before long. And on February 4, 1847, a rescue party left Johnson's Ranch.

Earlier, after Reed had regained his strength during November, he'd tried, with William McCutchen who had gone to California with Charles Stanton during the fall, to return and help the struggling party. The weather was too severe and with thirty horses, a mule and two Indians, the trip could not be made. The horses sank out of sight into bottomless drifts and he needed more men. When Reed returned to Sutter's settlement, he found nearly all the men gone off fighting the Mexicans. (The Mexican War had begun with the U.S. declaration of war in May 1846.) There was no one left to help him. Now when Reed got word that the first rescue party was on its way, he immediately set out with another party.

The rescue party from Johnson's Ranch had to send most of their horses back; the snow was still too deep. When they lightened their 75-pound packs, they stored nearly half of their load in trees and continued on into deeper and deeper snow. It took two weeks to cross the divide, and they rushed ahead, hoping to find living people, but fearing they would not.

The first camp they entered was brilliantly white and startlingly silent in its wintry setting. Someone remembered later that a craggy-faced woman, a shawl drawn tight around her bony shoulders, squinted at the glaring snow and squeaked, "Are you from Californy or from Heaven?"

And the rescuers found devastation. Thirteen were dead. Evidence of cannibalism was everywhere. At Alder Creek, George Donner was dying; his wife Tamsen stayed with him. The four strongest Donner children were made to leave with the first relief party.

There were 23 that left with the first group, but James Reed's two youngest, Tommy and Patty, were sent back because they were too weak. Patty, just eight years old, looked up and told her mother good-bye, then added, "Well, Mother, if you never see me again, do the best you can."

Of this trip over the mountains, Virginia wrote later, "We went over great hye mountain as strait as stair steps in snow up to our knees litle James walk the hole way over all the mountain in snow up to his waist. He said every step he took he was a gitting nigher Pa and something to eat."

The first party and the 21 pioneers they rescued met James Reed's rescue party just across the divide. Reed recorded in his diary for that day, February 27, 1847, "I met Mrs. Reed and two children still in the mountains. I cannot describe the death like look they all had." After a brief reunion with his family, Reed continued on leading his rescue party into the camp about March 1.

Matters had grown worse. Jacob Donner's body was being eaten by his children. Jacob's starving wife cooked him, but would not eat. George Donner, still alive, was too weak to travel. Reed gathered seventeen (mostly children) for the return trip, including his Tommy and Patty.

A third relief party led by William Foster and William Eddy arrived later in March and found Lewis Keseberg eating the flesh of

Foster's and Eddy's dead sons. Keseberg seemed near death, so they left him.

In April, a rescue party went after the last of the survivors. George and Tamsen Donner were dead. They found the demented Keseberg still alive and still eating human flesh. The newly melted snow revealed well-preserved parts of oxen that Kesseberg could have eaten, but he told the onlookers, "Oh! it's too dry eating!"

Eighty-two people had arrived at the foot of the Sierras in October 1846. Five had died on their way to the Sierras, 35 (14 children) more died in the mountains, along with two Indians sent to rescue them. Forty-seven made their way safely to California. James Reed wrote his brother-in-law: "The disasters of the company to which I belonged, should not deter any person from coming who wishes to try his fortune." It was this kind of optimism that led them from Springfield, Illinois in the spring of 1846 and it was that kind of optimism that led James Reed to become a prominent and wealthy Californian in the years that followed. He became San Jose's first pioneer real-estate developer. He died in 1874.

Mrs. Reed died in 1861. Their daughter Virginia married John M. Murphy, who came to California with the Stevens' Party in 1844, and he helped build an early real-estate business in California. She lived to age 86, dying in 1921.

Lewis Keseberg was 81 when he died in 1895 in a suburb of the Sacramento County Hospital. The last survivor, Isabella MacMahon, one of the Breen children, died March 25, 1935 in San Francisco.

In 1918, a monument was constructed at Donner Pass commemorating the ordeal that the Illinoisans and others had survived. Two of the Donner children were present, as was little Patty Reed. In the years since, a transcontinental railroad and Interstate 80 use the same route. Few travelers, however, will ever carry the spirit of a nation's greatness through the pass any better than that fated little group from Illinois during the terrible winter of 1846-1847.

Oh, and Lansford Hastings, the author of the Hastings Cutoff. His life was threatened by some. Nevertheless, he survived and eventually tried to set up a colony in Brazil for ex-Confederates. That was in the 1870s. Hastings died there.

In that May, 1847 letter written by Virginia Reed to her Springfield cousin, she wrote, "O Mary I have not rote you half of the truble we have had but I have rote you anuf to let you know that you dont now what truble is but thank god we have all got throw and the onely family that did not eat human flesh we have left everything but i don't cair for that we have got throw with our lives."

Virginia concluded, "Never take no cutofs and hury along as fast as you can."

DIARY OF DISASTER:
The Patrick Breen Diary

A portion of the diary published in the *Illinois State Journal*, September 16, 1847 follows:

Truckey's Lake, Nov. 20, 1846.

Came to this place on the 31st of last month; went into the Pass, the snow so deep we were unable to find the road. We now have killed most part of our cattle, having to remain here until next spring, and live on lean meat, without bread or salt.

Nov. 25—Cloudy; looks like the eve of a snow storm.

Nov. 26—Began to snow last evening; now rains or sleets.

Nov. 29—Still snowing; now about three feet deep; killed my last oxen to-day; gave another yoke to Foster; wood hard to be got.

Nov. 30—Snowing fast; no living things without wings can get about.

Dec. 1—Still snowing; wind west; snow about six or six and one-half feet deep; very difficult to get wood; our cattle all killed but two or three, and these, with the horses and Stanton's mules, all supposed to be lost in the snow; no hopes of finding them alive.

Dec. 3—Ceases snowing.

Dec. 4—Beautiful sunshine; snow seven or eight deep.

Dec. 8—Fine weather; hard work to find wood sufficient to keep us warm, or cook our beef.

Dec. 9—Commenced snowing; took in Spitzer yesterday, so weak that he cannot rise without help, caused by starvation. Some have a scant supply of beef.

Dec. 10—Continues to snow.

Dec. 14—Snows faster than any previous day.

Dec. 17—Bayless Williams died night before last; Milton and Noah not returned yet; think they are lost in the snow.

Dec. 20—Our hopes are in God; Amen.

Dec. 21—Sad news; Jacob Donner, Samuel Shoemaker, Rhinehart and Smith are dead; snowed all night.

Dec. 23—Began this day to read the "Thirty days' Prayers," Almighty God grant the requests of unworthy sinners!

Dec. 24—Rained all night and still continues; poor prospect for any kind of comfort, spiritual or temporal.

Dec. 25—Snowed all night and snows yet; extremely difficult to find wood, offered our prayers to God this, Christmas morning; the prospect is appalling, but we trust in Him.

Dec. 27—Wood growing scarcer; a tree, when felled, sinks into the snow, and is hard to be got at.

Dec. 30—Charles Berger died last evening.

Dec. 31—May we, with the help of God, spend the coming year better than we have the past; deliver us from our present dreadful situation; Amen. Looks like another snow storm; snow storms are dreadful to us.

Jan. 1, 1847—We pray the God of mercy to deliver us from our present calamity, if it be His holy will. Commenced snowing last night; provisions getting scant; dug up a hide from under the snow yesterday; have not commenced on it yet.

Jan. 3—Mrs. Reed talks of crossing the mountains with her children.

Jan. 4—Mrs. Reed and Virginia, Milton Elliot and Eliza Williams started a short time ago, with the hope of crossing the mountain.

Jan. 6—Eliza came back from the mountains yesterday evening.

Jan. 8—Mrs. Reed and others came back; they have nothing but hides to live on.

Jan. 13—Snowing fast; snow higher than the shanty; it must be thirteen feet deep; cannot get wood.

Jan. 14—Cleared off yesterday; praise be to the God of Heaven.

Jan. 15—Mrs. Murphy blind; Lanthron not able to get wood; it looks like another storm.

Jan. 17—Lanthron became crazy last night; provisions scarce; hides our main subsistence; may the Almighty send us help.

Jan. 21—John Battise and Mr. Denton came this morning with Eliza. She will not eat hides.

Jan. 22—Began to snow.

Jan. 23—Blew hard and snowed all night; the most severe storm we have experienced this winter.

Jan. 26—Provisions getting scant; people growing weak; living on small allowance of hides.

Jan. 28—Commenced snowing yesterday; food growing scarcer; don't have fire enough to cook our hides.

Jan. 30—Fair and pleasant.

Jan. 31—Lanthron Murphy died last night.

Feb. 5—Snowed hard; many uneasy for fear we shall all perish with hunger; we have but little meat left, and only three hides; Mrs. Reed has nothing but one hide; Eddy's child died last night.

Feb. 6—Murphy's folks and Kieseburg say they cannot eat hides; I wish we had enough of them; Mrs. Eddy is very weak.

Feb. 7—McCutcheon's child died on the second of this month.

Feb. 8—Spitzer died; we will bury him in the snow. Mrs. Eddy died on the night of the seventh.

Feb. 9—Mr. Pike's child all but dead; Milton is at Murphy's, not able to get out of bed; Mrs. Eddy and child were buried to-day.

Feb. 10—Milton Eddy died last night; all are entirely out of meat; our hides are nearly all eat up; with God's help spring will soon smile upon us.

Feb. 14—Fine morning, but cold; buried Milton in the snow. John Denton not well.

Feb. 16—We all feel very unwell.

Feb. 19—Seven men arrived from California yesterday evening with provisions.

Feb. 22—Buried Pike's child this morning in the snow; it died two days ago.

Feb. 23—Shot a dog to-day, and dressed his flesh.

Feb. 25—The wolves are about to dig up the dead bodies around our shanty; we hear them howl.

Feb. 26—Hungry times in camp; plenty of hides, but the folks wont eat them; Mrs. Murphy said here yesterday, that she thought she would commence on Milton and eat him; I do not think she has done so yet; it is distressing.

Feb. 28—One solitary Indian passed by yesterday; gave me five or six roots, resembling onions in shape; tasted some like a sweet potato.

Feb. 29—Ten men arrived this morning from Bear Valley, with provisions. We all leave in two or three days.

AN INCOMPLETE LIST
of those with the
DONNER-REED PARTY

From Springfield, Illinois:

Reed, James Frazier	*Donner, George
Mrs. Margaret W.	*Mrs. Tamsen
Virginia E. Backenstoe	Elitha C.
(Mrs. Reed's daughter)	Leanna C.
Martha J.(Patty)	Francis E.
James F., Jr.	Georgiana

Thomas K.
*Mrs. Sarah Keyes
  (Mrs. Reed's mother)
*Donner, Jacob

*Mrs. Elizabeth
*Isaac
*Lewis
*Samuel
George
Mary M.
*William Hook
  (Mrs. Donner's son)
Solomon E. Hook
  (Mrs. Donner's son)

Eliza P.

*Milford Elliot
*James Smith
*John Denton
Noah James
Eliza Williams
*Baylis Williams
Walter Herron
Hiram O. Miller
(Took Fort Hall route)

The Following Joined Later:

From Lacon, Illinois:

*Fausdick, Jay
Mrs. Sarah (daugther of F.W. Graves)
*Graves, Franklin Ward ("Uncle Billy")
Mrs. Elizabeth
Mary Ann
*Franklin
William C.
Eleanor
Jonathan B.
*John Snyder

Nancy
Elizabeth, Jr.
Franklin Ward, Jr.
Lavina

From Iowa:

Breen, Patrick
Mrs. Margaret
Isabella
John
Patrick, Jr.
James

*Patrick Dolan

Edward J.
Simon P.
Peter

From Belleville, Illinois:

Eddy, William H.
*Mrs. Eleanor
*James P.
*Baby

From Ray County, Missouri:
McCutchen, William ("Mac")
Mrs. Amanda
*Harriet

From Tennessee:
*Murphy, Mrs. Lavina (widow)
*John Landrum (son)   William M. Pike
*Lemuel B.   (Mrs. Murphy's son-in-law)
Mary M.   Mrs. Harriet Murphy
William G.   Naomi L.
                              Catherine

From St. Louis, Missouri:
Foster, William M.
   (Mrs. Murphy's son-in-law)
Mrs. Sarah Murphy
*George

From Germany:
Keseberg, Lewis   *Wolfinger, Mr. ——
Mrs. Phillipine   Mrs. ——
Ada
Lewis, Jr.
*Reinhardt, Joseph   *Spitzer, Augustus
*Burger, Karl ("Dutch Charley")

From Springfield, Ohio:
*Shoemaker, Samuel

From Chicago, Illinois:
*Stanton, Charles Tyler

From Belgium:
*Hardkoop, Mr. ——

Miscellaneous others:
*Halloran, Luke

4

Real Woman—
The Fanny Kelly Story

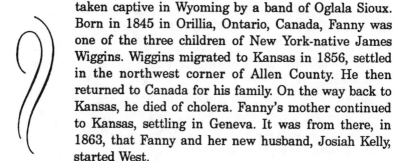

It has been nearly 125 years since 19-year-old Fanny Kelly was taken captive in Wyoming by a band of Oglala Sioux. Born in 1845 in Orillia, Ontario, Canada, Fanny was one of the three children of New York-native James Wiggins. Wiggins migrated to Kansas in 1856, settled in the northwest corner of Allen County. He then returned to Canada for his family. On the way back to Kansas, he died of cholera. Fanny's mother continued to Kansas, settling in Geneva. It was from there, in 1863, that Fanny and her new husband, Josiah Kelly, started West.

Fanny's best-selling account, *Narrative of My Captivity among the Sioux Indians,* was published first in 1871 and reprinted 10 times over the next 20 years. More than anything, her story reveals the strength, character and courage of the 19th Century pioneer woman.

A raw north wind tugged at the Indian clothing Real Woman wore. It was a bitterly cold day and her clothing was tattered and worn. She pulled a shawl tighter around her cold raw cheeks. Her eyes teared from the wind and morning light, but through her clouded eyes she saw Fort Sully just ahead. And she saw soldiers standing on rooftops. The Flag of the United States floated proudly over the stockade walls. Her heart pounded.

Ahead of her, their shaggy ponies stepping carefully over the frozen earth, rode eight painted Sioux chiefs, all singing songs, one leading the horse she rode. Behind her rode the warriors. All together, perhaps 1,000 mounted Sioux came closer to the fort. In the distance, she could see the Missouri River.

From the fort, an Indian walked toward the Sioux riders. The fort gate opened and an Army major, A.E. House, stepped out. Several officers and an interpreter followed along behind House. When they reached the riders, the interpreter began the conversation. The woman the Sioux called Real Woman waited, wondering what it was all about.

A captain, John Logan, Company K, a kind-faced man, approached Real Woman. She watched him, afraid to ask the question that burned in her mind and heart. But then gasping, she asked, "Am I free, indeed free?"

The captain's eyes filled with tears as he nodded, and scarcely audibly, said, "Yes."

Moments later, Real Woman, Fanny Kelly was inside the fort, safe and sound, a free woman for the first time in five months.

It had all started for the 19-year-old Fanny Kelly in the spring of 1864. In November 1863, she had married Civil War veteran Josiah S. Kelly. Mr. Kelly was not well. The Kansas climate did not agree with him so they packed and headed for Idaho.

With them, on May 17, 1864, when they rolled out of Geneva, Kansas, in Allen County, was their adopted daughter, Mary, Fanny's sister's 5-year-old daughter. A friend, Gardner Wakefield, and the Kelly's two colored servants, Franklin and Andy came along too.

A few days later, they were joined by a Methodist minister, the Reverend Mr. Sharp. And soon they caught up with William J. Larimer, his wife Sarah and their eight-year-old son, also from Allen County. This made a total of 10 in the party. Soon a Mr. Taylor joined, making a total of 11 people and five wagons.

It was like a family outing for the next several weeks. The days were hot, but the evenings wonderfully cool. Each day, Mr. Kelly rode ahead to find a campsite and the servants, Franklin and Andy, made camp.

Fanny, Mary and the others sometimes picked berries on arrival, then after supper, they sang, read or wrote letters. Often they merely talked about the beautiful things they had seen along the way.

Fanny loved the prairie flowers: "Yellow, purple, white, and blue, making the earth look like a rich carpet of variegated colors." She recalled the brilliance of the lightning storms: "A gleam of lightning, like a forked tongue of flame, shot out of all the black clouds, blinding us."

There were hardships, but not many. She complained about cooking with buffalo chips. She was frightened when they lashed four wagon boxes together and 20 men rowed them across the Platte River. That took four days.

The wagon train met Indians from time to time, but all were friendly. They passed the site of the Blue Water Fight where the Army avenged the killing of Lt. J.L. Gratten and then within days, they drove their wagons up to Fort Laramie.

Assured that the Indians west of the fort were friendly, they hitched their teams and rolled west. Then about 80 miles from the fort on Tuesday, July 12, 1864, in the valley of the Little Box Elder in the foothills of Wyoming's Laramie Range, they ran head on into trouble.

Near sunset someone noticed Indians on a nearby bluff. Fanny remembered that there must have been 250 of them. And they were "painted and equipped for war."

The men quickly ordered that the wagons be "corralled." Josiah Kelly was in charge and Fanny called to him, "If you fire one shot, I feel sure you will seal our fate, as they seem to outnumber us ten to one, and will at once massacre all of us."

Shortly, the Indians, Oglala Sioux, rode toward them. Mr. Kelly mounted his sleek thoroughbred and rode to meet them outside the wagons. The war chief told Kelly they were hunting. They were friends, they insisted, and made a point of shaking hands. Others of the Sioux came down. They admired Kelly's mount. Did he want to trade the horse?

Kelly was not interested, but he offered them flour. They begged for clothing and gave Fanny a pair of beaded moccasins. All the time, Fanny noticed, the Indians "grew bolder and more insolent."

One warrior grabbed at Mr. Kelly's gun, but Kelly would not turn it loose. Then to everyone's surprise the head man of the Sioux came to Kelly and said they would not be bothered; they could go. Tensions eased some. Just an hour had passed since they first spotted the Sioux on the bluffs. The wagons moved again, rolling toward a rocky glen, the Sioux still in sight. A short time later, Kelly, fearing an ambush, ordered the five wagons halted. Most of the Indians rode on, but some remained. Franklin and Andy, the black servants, were told to prepare supper for the Sioux.

William Larimer and Franklin prepared a fire while Josiah Kelly and Andy walked away from the wagons to gather wood. Wakefield unloaded provisions from his wagon. Taylor tended his team. Reverend Sharp was busy passing out sugar to the Sioux.

Suddenly, it happened. No one remembered the exact sequence of events, but Taylor dropped, a rifle ball through his forehead. Reverend Sharp died. Franklin lay by the fire, his body full of arrows. Wakefield was down, mortally wounded.

Then the Indians tore at the wagons, destroying, ripping, splitting, tomahawks flying and slashing. At Fanny Kelly's wagon, two warriors dragged her to the ground. She held Mary, begging for mercy. The Sioux headman touched the revolver he had jammed into his belt and signed for her to be quiet.

Just then, in the distance, a wagon appeared. Several of the Sioux mounted their ponies and charged off in a cloud of dust. They killed a man off the wagon, but the others managed to escape.

In the meantime, the Sioux led little Mary and Fanny away from the wagons. Mrs. Larimer was with them. She cried, "The men have all escaped, and left us to the mercy of the savages."

Fanny said she hoped so. "They would be killed," she scolded, "and then all hope of rescue of us would be at an end." Mrs. Larimer screamed. The Sioux dragged her photographic equipment onto the ground. It was her Daguerro equipment. She planned to become a photographer in Idaho. Because of the screaming, the warriors threatened her. Fanny tried to calm her. The headman came up and placed a "feathered wreath" on Fanny's head,

In this drawing from Kelly's My Captivity Among the Sioux Indians, *she shows fear and terror of her captives.*
(Author's Collection)

then left her, Mrs. Larimer and Mary under guard. Maybe they would not be killed.

The long July day was ending, but the Sioux continued to plunder the wagons. One warrior brought clothes to the women. Another came with letters, books and papers. Others piled odds and ends from the wagons and then set it all afire.

Just after dark, the Sioux brought them horses. Fanny mounted, Mary on behind. A warrior took a lead rein and Fanny held a rein that was tied to the horse's lower jaw. Fanny and Mary were led out of Wyoming's Little Box Elder valley and into the night.

While all this activity went on in the camp, Josiah Kelly was without a gun while collecting wood. Larimer, wounded by an arrow, fled into the timber and Kelly hid in sage grass. Andy was with Kelly and they worked their way east to find help. After a while, they returned to the scene only to find the bodies of Sharp, Taylor and Franklin. Franklin's legs were pinned together with an arrow. His head was bashed in. Gardner Wakefield's body was found about one-quarter mile away. He was pierced with three arrows.

The cattle stood nearby, but the Sioux had taken all the horses. Kelly figured they had better travel on to Deer Creek Station for help. They were only 12 miles from the tiny outpost.

At Deer Creek, Kelly telegraphed Fort Laramie. Colonel Collins, of the 11th Ohio Cavalry, ordered Captains Shuman and Marshall and two companies out against the Sioux. The soldiers rode out the 100 miles from Fort Laramie and searched for three days, with the loss of a lieutenant named Brown. Fanny Kelly claimed later that Brown was killed when he and Josiah tried to talk to an Indian village they had discovered.

Her first night with the Sioux was beautiful and starlit, Fanny recalled later. The night was full of sound. There was rippling water over rocks in the distance, night birds crying out in the cool night air, and insects chirping at the dark.

They rode north out of the bottomland and onto some bluffs. The Sioux chanted songs as they rode through the night.

All this time, Fanny was plotting escape. She dropped letters, marking the trail. She was determined to free Mary first. She told little Mary to follow the letters back to the wagons. She whispered, "Drop gently down, and lie on the ground for a while." She added, "Then retrace your steps. If I can, I will follow you."

Little Mary dropped silently to the ground, Fanny's horse never breaking stride. Fanny waited breathlessly. The Indians had not noticed!

In a while, she too slipped off. She hugged the ground as the Sioux continued on. Then they were gone! But not for long. For before she could retreat, she heard a commotion. Suddenly out of the night, the Sioux returned. Forty or 50 warriors rode side by side, sweeping the area along the path.

As the Indian ponies neared her they spooked and reared. She stood and explained that Mary must have fallen asleep and fell from her horse. She was only looking for the little girl, she lied.

They would send a search party for Mary at first light, the Sioux promised. (Fanny never saw Mary again. Josiah Kelly and a search party did find her later, not far from the wagons, pinioned to the ground with arrows. She had been scalped. Fanny suspected as much as weeks after her capture, she saw a "bright, little shawl" and a "fair-haired scalp" in the possession of a young warrior.)

By dawn, Fanny's horse was weaving along through a maze of craggy peaks and rugged ravines. She heard water and then they swam the North Platte, still northbound.

Just across the river, the band split. Fanny's group trailed off north by northwest, as closely as she could figure, eventually striking the Powder River near where Fort Reno was to stand. They crossed Deer Fork, Rock Creek, Crazy Woman's Fork and Clear Creek. During this time, she saw only Indians, except on one occasion she saw Mrs. Larimer. But they were not together long and, unknown to Fanny, Mrs. Larimer and her eight-year-old son soon escaped.

Fanny recalled seeing all kinds of wildlife. She remembered herds of buffalo stampeding in front of a prairie fire, the earth trembling beneath her feet. She saw elk, black- and white-tailed deer, antelope, sage hens, prairie chickens, geese, brants, ducks, beaver, otter, fish, wolves and "grizzly and cinnamon bears."

By the last week of July, the Sioux were at their main camp near the Tongue River in Montana. The village "stretched for miles along the banks of the stream," she recalled.

During her stay with the Indians, she lived in the lodge of an Oglala headman she called Ottawa. To the Sioux, he was known as Brings-Plenty. Fanny remembered him as "very old, over seventy-five, partially blind, and very ferocious and savage looking."

Her experiences over the next months were varied. She helped prepare Indian tobacco called kinnikinnick—a willow bark and tobacco mixture. She remembered, "I had been obliged to paint daily, like the rest of my companions, and narrowly escaped tattooing, by pretending to faint away every time the implements for the marring operation were applied."

She had trouble understanding the Indians: "I was constantly annoyed, worried and terrified by their strange conduct...I knew not how to get along with them. I always tried to please them, and was as cheerful as I could be under the circumstances, for my own sake." After a while, she did learn enough of their language to understand much of what went on.

On one occasion, Fanny's life was threatened. Some of the Sioux thought she should be killed to compensate for the deaths of battle losses. Brings-Plenty interceded on her behalf: "Why should we punish the innocent for the guilty?"

There were other captives among the Sioux that she met from time to time. One was Mary Boyeau, called Madee. She was a victim of the Spirit Lake fight. Fanny remembered that she was "a fair-faced, beautiful young girl." She was married to a Yankton Sioux.

On another occasion she met a girl stolen 25 years earlier from an Oregon-bound wagon train. She saw a 14-year-old from Quincy, Illinois named Charles Sylvester. He had been among the Indians for seven years, she claimed.

And she reported seeing other victims of this clash of cultures. She met mixed-blood children. One mother of such a child said she had been the wife of a captain at Fort Laramie until his white wife arrived from the East. The woman's child was dressed in military clothes and had a fair complexion. Fanny said, "I saw many other fair-faced little children, and heard the sad story from their mothers."

There were occasions when she thought she might be freed. In August, an Indian named Porcupine brought her a letter from Capt. Levi G. Marshall of Company E, 11th Ohio Cavalry. Marshall explained that he had tried to find her but failed. Porcupine was to talk to Brings-Plenty, but the old man was not ready to give her up.

Early in September, Capt. James L. Fisk commanding an escort and 100 wagons came very near the Sioux camp. Somehow a note was sent to the train. The soldiers refused to believe the message. Another note assured the wagons and soldiers that there was indeed a white woman in the Sioux camp. To prove it, she stood on a hill; the soldiers saw her through binoculars.

One of the men in the train offered $800 for ransom, but Captain Fisk was still fearful. Fisk finally offered three wagonloads of goods for her, but she too feared the Sioux were planning a trick and wrote to Fisk saying as much. Nevertheless, Fisk spread the word that she was alive. Fanny remembered, someone in the train who had lost relatives in the Minnesota Uprising poisoned a box of crackers with strychnine and left it where the Indians would find it. They did; they died. According to Fanny, "The Indians told me afterward that more had died from eating bad bread than from bullets during the whole summer campaign."

The unrest that began with the Minnesota war in 1862 had spilled over into the plains in 1863 and 1864. The soldiers had been out on the plains and there were skirmishes, even with the band in which Fanny was held.

There were other rescue attempts. Young Colonel Charles A.R. Dimon, rode out of Fort Rice in December looking for Fanny Kelly. He rode a 40-mile circuit in temperatures that dropped to 34 degrees below zero. Several of his men suffered "frozen feet, faces, and fingers." (After she was freed, Dimon rode for nine days to Fort Sully to see Kelly and pick up supplies.)

While Fanny remained captive, her husband, Josiah Kelly, began sending agency Indians out, searching for her. Kelly eventually offered 19 horses for her safe return, but when there were no results he returned east to Fort Leavenworth for the winter. He hoped to raise an independent company to search for Fanny.

Fanny wrote later, "During the last weeks of my captivity, the Indians had done all in their power for me, all their circumstances and condition would allow, and the women were very kind, but 'their people were not my people,' and I was detained a captive, far from home, and friends, and civilization."

Early in December 1864, a large company of Blackfeet Sioux on a very cold day, rode into the Grand River valley and stopped at Laughing Wood where the Hunkpapa camp was (near Bullhead, near the mouth of Rock Creek). Crawler led this group and announced that he was there to buy Real Woman. (Brings-Plenty named Fanny, Real Woman, a title of honor "reserved for women of the most unquestioned character.")

But Brings-Plenty had other ideas. He planned on trading her, Brings-Plenty claimed, but not for the horses Crawler offered. Brings-Plenty took Fanny and went inside his lodge.

Crawler and his group stood outside. Sitting Bull, the Hunkpapa Sioux medicine man, was in this camp and he came to the lodge and said loud enough for all to hear, "Friends, this woman is out of our path. Her path is different. You can see in her face that she is homesick and unhappy here. So I'm going to send her back."

Sitting Bull looked at Crawler and said, "Go in and get her. And tell him I said so."

When Crawler entered, Brings-Plenty sat opposite the doors behind the fire. Fanny was on his left. Crawler warmed his hands, then said, "I have come for this woman."

Brings-Plenty, staring at the fire, said, "I have no use for your horses. I will keep the captive."

Crawler, still rubbing his hands, said, "My friend, I would advise you to exchange the captive for the horses."

Brings-Plenty replied, "My friend, I have no desire to part with the captive."

Crawler eased closer to the fire and closer to Fanny as he asked again, and was refused. Brings-Plenty's knife lay by his side now. Crawler suddenly surprised Fanny and Brings-Plenty by drawing a revolver from his belt and pointing at Brings-Plenty's face. Grabbing Fanny by the shoulder, he pulled her past and behind him.

Then, the pistol still aimed at Brings-Plenty's face, he backed out of the lodge door.

Outside, the Sioux put Fanny on a horse. The crowd of Hunkpapa watched this. Some seemed to approve of their cousins' actions; others did not like it. Sitting Bull, sensing this, designated several Hunkpapa men to accompany Crawler and the Blackfeet Sioux to protect Fanny. Sitting Bull told them, "Care for her well. Choose good men to see that no harm comes to her."

This incident was of particular importance to the Hunkpapa. Their winter-count calendar calls the winter of 1864-65 "The-Winter-When-the-White-Woman-was-Rescued."

Over the next days, Fanny traveled with Crawler's family as they made their way toward Fort Sully. Finally at the fort, a young Sioux later named John Grass, took a letter Fanny had written to the fort. She warned that the Indians planned to overrun the fort.

That, however, did not turn out to be the case. Instead, they camped peacefully outside for a few days and then returned to their homes. On one occasion, the Sioux invited her to come out of the fort and eat with them, but she did not acknowledge their invitation.

Fanny was not in good health. The raw antelope meat often eaten in the open, the terrible storms she had endured, and the poor condition of the clothing that she and

Fanny Kelly passes a message to a friend who is to warn of an Indian attack on the Army. (From My Captivity Among the Sioux Indians.*)*

(Author's Collection)

the Sioux wore left her weak and emaciated. Her limbs and hands and face were frozen. For the next several weeks she remained in the hospital at Fort Sully.

Early in February 1865, Josiah came for her and they returned to Kansas. Together, they ran a hotel in Ellsworth until Josiah died during the cholera epidemic of 1867. Fanny, although deathly ill and pregnant at the time with their son, survived.

She sold the hotel and in 1868, at the invitation of William and Sarah Larimer, friends from the wagon train, moved to Sherman, Wyoming Territory, on the Union Pacific Railroad between Cheyenne and Laramie. One that remembered her from those days said, "Fanny Kelly was a pitiful person eking out a living here at Sherman by taking in washings for the railroad crews."

Friends all along had urged that she make a claim to the U.S. Government for her losses in the Indian raid. Most agreed that the Kellys were due something. In 1869 she traveled to Washington, D.C. to try to see President U.S. Grant.

She lived in Washington, D.C. the rest of her life. Eventually, she was paid from tribal allotments for her personal and property losses and deprivations. Other records indicate that she received $5,000 from Congress in April 1870 for her service in saving Captain James L. Fisk's train and Fort Sully.

With the book, these payments, a government job and wise investments, she apparently did well financially. She had retained the family holdings at Geneva, Kansas, and that also became a source of income for her.

On May 5, 1880, Fanny married a Kansas journalist named William F. Gordon. Together, they lived in Washington, D.C. until her death on November 15, 1904. Her death was attributed to a cerebral hemorrhage. She was interred in Glenwood Cemetery.

A brave, resourceful woman, Fanny Kelly Gordon never seemed to let down. Hard work and faith in herself carried her from one hardship to another until her life ended peacefully nearly six decades after it began.

5

Frances Grummond and the Indians

Wyoming skies were never clearer, nor air colder and drier than on December 21, 1866, the Friday before Christmas. It was a beautiful, bright day. There had been snow, but it was mostly melted now, except for that in shaded areas.

Columns of white smoke climbed slowly above the big, new fort and a column of soldiers and wagons trailed away toward trees in the distance. It was the woodcutting detail.

A short distance from Fort Phil Kearny and out of sight, about 2,000 Indian warriors prepared a trap. Everything was as they planned it. They were young men of the Cheyenne, Arapaho and Sioux nations. They had watched these Bluecoat soldiers for several moons now. They had decided they could kill many of these Bluecoats with an ambush and the ambush was ready.

North of the fort along Peno Creek on the downside of a north slope, the Arapaho and Cheyenne took their positions on the west side of the creek. The other side was flatter, but several Sioux found enough grass to hide in. Others waited nearby, mounted and ready to charge at the soldiers. Ten young men picked from the Cheyenne, Arapahoes, and Sioux made up the decoys. Crazy Horse, the Oglala Sioux, was one. Hump and Little Wolf were also leaders of this special group of 10. The decoys' mission was dangerous and depended on timing.

Another group of young warriors waited in hiding to attack the Bluecoat woodcutters. When Crazy Horse and the other decoys heard the gunfire from the attack on the woodcutters, it was time for them to act. Just as they figured, when the popping of the guns began, a column of soldiers dashed out of the fort to the rescue of the woodcutting detail.

As soon as the soldiers rode out of sight, Crazy Horse kicked his pony into the open and began waving a red Hudson Bay blanket at the fort. The other decoys joined him and rode back and forth, taunting the soldiers. Even when the soldiers in the fort shot at them, they continued taunting and riding around, zigzagging their ponies, inviting the soldiers to chase them.

And then, just like the warriors planned it, the gates swung open again. This time, out came more soldiers, some mounted, others on foot. They headed straight toward Crazy Horse and the nine brave young warriors, the only Indians visible from the fort.

Ever so slowly, Crazy Horse led the decoys back toward Lodge Trail Ridge. The soldiers from the fort chased them. And when the decoys were on the ridge, they rode down toward Peno Creek. The Bluecoat soldiers, still hot for a fight, charged after them. The trap was nearly sprung

Back in the fort, the pregnant Frances Grummond waited with the other women who had followed their soldier husbands half-way across the continent to this Indian-infested, frontier outpost. Frances Grummond's husband was chasing the decoys, but it was not unusual for him to ride into the face of death. It happened often here. As a matter of fact, it had been that way here from the start.

Just three months earlier, Frances Grummond and her husband, U.S. Army Lt. George Washington Grummond, arrived in the middle of a another raid on the wood train. An escort rode out over the grassy hills and led the Grummonds safely to the fort, but not before they stood aside and watched in horror as an Army wagon entered the fort in front of them with a stripped and scalped, dead soldier as cargo.

"Let me get within the gate!" she thought.

Actually the trip from the East had been enjoyable. Frances Courtney (known affectionately as Miss Fanny) had married Lt. Grummond shortly after the Civil War. He was a captain in a Michigan Volunteer Infantry regiment and was in Frances' hometown of Franklin, Tennessee when they met. Later, he achieved the rank of lieutenant colonel and received a brevet to brigadier general for action at the Battle of Bentonville, North Carolina.

When the war ended, Grummond entered the regular Army with a second lieutenant's commission. He and Miss Fanny Courtney were married on September 3, 1865, just a few months after her sister, Florence, married a Union officer, Lt. Jim Crochnour of New York.

(The Courtneys, for some reason, were Union sympathizers. Following the Battle of Franklin on November 30, 1864, Mrs. Robert Courtney and her daughters attended the Union wounded in the Presbyterian Church at Franklin. Strangely, at the same time, their son and brother, William Wirt Courtney, was fighting for the Confederate cause.)

Lt. Grummond was assigned to Col. Henry Beebe Carrington's 18th U.S. Infantry. He and his bride were posted to Governor's Island, New York Harbor, then later ordered to Vicksburg.

They spent the hot summer of 1866 in Mississippi before being ordered west to Wyoming. From Vicksburg, with a detail of recruits, the Grummonds traveled by steamboat to St. Louis, Fort Leavenworth and Omaha. After a train ride, they switched to an ambulance. Their nights were sometimes spent at ranches. At other times, they slept in the ambulance on straw pillows and gray Army blankets. Finally, they passed Fort Sedgwick and Fort Laramie and were on their way to Fort Phil Kearny.

Frances Grummond saw the Bighorn Mountains and from 80 miles away and on Monday, September 17, the Grummonds rode within sight of their destination. She wrote later, "I could have clapped my hands for joy, but that would not have adequately expressed my experience, which was that of a far deeper current of emotions beyond the province of mere words to express."

At the fort, "a place of refuge from fatigue and danger," she called it, they had no permanent quarters, but two "A" tents were set up for them. Her trunks and "two rather dilapidated camp stools and a disfigured mess-chest" stayed in the front tent. In the rear tent, there stood two hospital bunks and a small stove. Back of that, a cook stove stood under a tarpaulin. It snowed that first night in this high country, but the Grummonds were safe and warm.

In the next days, Frances Grummond learned why the fort was located there in northern Wyoming. Gold discovered in Montana, for some, was the reason. Miners and businessmen at Virginia City wanted a safe trail east. A 27-year-old gold miner named John M. Bozeman from Coweta County, Georgia was hired to mark a trail. With him went John M. Jacobs.

The two men left Virginia City, Montana and worked their way east and then south to the Oregon Trail. Their trail crossed the Continental Divide only once and stayed away from mountain roads. It passed into Wyoming east of the Big Horn Mountains and continued southeast through the Powder River Basin toward present Douglas, Wyoming, where it joined the Oregon Trail.

But there was one tragic fault. The Bozeman Trail passed through the heart of Oglala and Minneconjou Sioux, Cheyenne and Arapaho country. The trail violated the last and best hunting grounds of these tribes, the 123,000 square miles promised them by the Fort Laramie Treaty of 1851 and by a renewed and revised version of the treaty in 1865.

With determination to keep the Bozeman Road open and despite a warning from the Oglala Sioux Chief Red Cloud that he would "mark every mile of that Bozeman Trail from the North Platte to the Yellowstone with the bodies of your soldiers," Col. Henry Carrington built Fort Phil Kearny. A Civil War veteran and Yale graduate, Col. Carrington and the 18th U.S. Infantry built the palisaded fort between the Little Piney and Big Piney Creeks, about 21 miles south of present Sheridan, Wyoming.

And now Frances Grummond heard just how serious the Indian problem was. Col. Carrington's wife, Margaret, told stories of the recent, horrible death of a soldier not far from the fort. And a correspondent for Frank Leslie's Illustrated Weekly also lost his scalp and life near the fort. The young man was with a hay-making party and decided to stop off and draw sketches of the area. He figured the Indians would not bother him. Later, when they found him, he was dead with a cross cut on his breast. That indicated the Indians thought he was a coward because he would not resist them.

The other women, Lt. William Bisbee's wife and Lt. Alexander Wand's wife, had Indian stories, too. So did other wives at the fort.

And if that was not enough, even the famous Jim Bridger, at the fort working for the Army, caused uneasiness. She wrote, "Bridger would walk about, constantly scanning the opposite hills that commanded a good view of the fort as if he suspected Indians of having scouts behind every sage clump or fallen cottonwood."

In the meantime, the Grummonds tried to get on with their lives. They soon moved into a large hospital tent that had been occupied by the Carringtons. Col. Carrington's family moved into the half-finished headquarters. The Grummonds found their new tent warmer and with better cooking facilities.

A few weeks later, they moved into a three-room house of recently-cut pine logs. The roof was pine poles covered with clay. Frances Grummond fashioned window shades of newspaper and sheeting, and the company tailor sewed gunnysacks for carpeting.

Food at the fort was satisfactory, although the "rather ancient" butter from the sutler's store was salty. She paid 75 cents a pound for it and kneaded hot water into it to make it edible. Milk was scarce because the Indians ran their cows off from time to time. She was able to get an "occasional" egg.

Always, however, Frances Grummond's attention was drawn back to the Indians. She often scanned the surrounding mountains, thinking how beautiful this place was. But then her eyes would be drawn to lonely Pilot Hill where the lives of those in the fort depended on an Army picket on lookout for Indians.

Since the stockade was not yet complete, she often wondered why the Indians did not attack. Slowly, the soldiers cut heavy pine trunks 11 feet long. These logs were, she wrote, "hewn to a touching surface of four inches, so as to join closely, all pointed, loop-holed, and imbedded in the ground for four feet." With all this, she was nearly always concerned about an Indian attack.

Once the fort was completed, she wrote, "My constant fear was that the Indians would work their way over the stockade under the cover of the darkness at night."

At night, hungry wolves gathered around the quartermaster's slaughter yard outside the stockade and near the Little Piney Creek. The yard drew the ravenous wolves because of the fresh blood and bits of flesh on the ground there. Were they not really Indians howling like that? Sixty-two-year-old Jim Bridger told her that wolf calls by Indians had no echo. Was there an echo to these calls?

One night, the Army tried to decoy the Indians into a nighttime ambush by placing mules where the Indians could get to them. The Indians were not deceived, but when the ambushers gave up and went to sleep, the Indians slipped in at daylight and stole Army cattle.

On another night, there was more reason for Frances Grummond and the others to be upset. On the Sullivant Hills, just northwest of the fort, the Indians built a huge fire. From the fort, the soldiers could see them dancing around the flickering flames. This time, Col. Carrington ordered three howitzer caseshots lobbed at the fire. The Indians extinguished the fire and disappeared north of the hills. In the daytime, life was busy inside the fort. The women were often "baking, brewing, stewing and sewing," Frances wrote. On Sundays, the Rev. David White, a Methodist chaplain, conducted services, and there was Sunday evening singing at headquarters.

Also on Sundays, the Wyoming night was filled with songs played by the band. These people on this little "island" in the middle of danger heard "Old Hundred," "Nearer My God to Thee," "Annie Laurie," and "When the Swallows Homeward Fly."

One of the more festive days that fall was a balmy, sunny October 31. The fort was nearly complete. The officers and men of the fort turned out, all 360 of them. New uniforms were issued to the men, and the officers wore their plumed, dress hats. In the distance, the slopes of the Big Horns, covered with the golden leaves of aspens, looked as if they, too, were dressed for the ceremony. The occasion was the raising of the flag. Col. Carrington, in a speech to all gathered there, noted that the Army had lost eight men since construction began in the summer. But there was much for the colonel and his men to be proud of. In the 15 weeks since they had begun this project, over 1,000 pioneers had passed safely along the Bozeman Road this past summer and fall. In special ceremonies that included firing the howitzers, the American flag was hoisted on the 124-foot flagpole, the first full Garrison Flag, to float between the Platte and Montana, according to Frances Grummond. The band played "The Star Spangled Banner."

At 3 o'clock that afternoon, Indians suddenly appeared. They had not been close by for three weeks. Out of the Sullivant Hills they rode and nearly to the fort's west gate before anyone noticed. Margaret Carrington remembered, "Others appeared upon the hills, and flashing mirrors were constantly passing signals for nearly an hour." Extra ammunition was issued to the men, but the threat passed, and by sundown, the Indians had vanished as mysteriously as they had appeared. There had, indeed, been great progress at Fort Phil Kearny in the four months, but this daring episode by the Indians reminded everyone that there was plenty more left to do at the Fort.

Col. Carrington had asked for more men in August. The Army said he would get them. He had also asked for more equipment. The Army said he would get it. But now in October, neither had arrived. An inspection revealed that many of his men's Civil War-issue Springfield rifles were worn out. Lt. Grummond's company, for example, claimed 26 Springfields, at the October inspection. Twenty of the weapons were unfit for use. In addition, the horses and mules at the fort were suffering from overstrain.

Then, in November, Company C, 2nd U.S. Cavalry, under the command of Lt. Horatio S. Bingham arrived. Half of Bingham's men were recruits, and they, too, were armed with the muzzle-loading Springfields. (A note on the Springfield rifle-musket: walnut stock and all, it was 58.5 inches long, weighed 9 1/4 pounds and fired a .58 caliber three-ring lead minie bullet that weighed 500 grains. But, as one Illinois Cavalry major pointed out during the Civil War, "After the first volley (the Springfields) were about as serviceable to a cavalryman ... as a good club." And a teamster at Fort Phil Kearny commented, "What show has a man with the old-fashioned Springfield musket? One shot and you are done.") And with Lt. Bingham came Captain William J. Fetterman. Since Capt. Fetterman had seniority over Capt. Tenodor Ten Eyck, Fetterman took over the 2nd Battalion of the 18th Infantry Regiment. Other than that, Fort Phil Kearny received no more reinforcements in November. On the other hand, the Indians increased their numbers in November. And they stepped up their harassment of the fort.

Then it was December. The month had a good beginning when Lt. Wilbur F. Arnold and 43 infantry recruits marched in from Fort Laramie, arriving on December 3. Three days later, however, on December 6, there was a problem. It was a bitter, cold day with a biting north wind. The wood train, out early, was attacked about 9 o'clock. Capt. Fetterman and 40 men rode to the sound of the gunfire to relieve the wagons, while Col. Carrington and Lt. Grummond led a mounted squad—24 men—north and around the Sullivant Hills to try to cut off the retreating Indians.

The Indians Fetterman chased turned on him, and Carrington's command faced attack by another group of Indians. With bugles blaring and horses thundering over frozen ground and through icy streams, there was confusion everywhere. Some of the horseback fighters were separated from their units, while others seemed to have been drawn off by Indians urging them toward one trap or another. Finally, Fetterman and Carrington reunited their commands and retreated back to the fort, but not before Lt. Horatio Bingham and Sgt. G.R. Bowers were killed. (Bingham's body was found with 50 arrows in it; Sgt. Bowers' skull was split with a hatchet.)

Frances Grummond's husband was in this fight and had escaped only when he "shut his eyes and literally slashed his way out." That night, when he was safely back at the fort, she wrote, "We both sat for a long time in silence, then mingled our tears in gratitude for the wonderful deliverance ... he said that he abandoned the use of spurs and jammed his sword into the weary beast to urge him to greater effort, followed by the chief, in full war-dress, with spear at his back so near that but for his good horse, he would then and there have met a terrible fate .... A sense of apprehension that I seemed to have been conscious of ever since my arrival at the post, deepened from that hour. No sleep came to my weary eyes, except fitfully, for many nights, and even then in my dreams I could see him riding madly from me with the Indians in pursuit."

And she was not the only one concerned at what was happening. Old Jim Bridger noted what was occurring, too. He was concerned about the Indians and the soldiers sent to fight them. On one occasion, he told Col. Carrington, "Your men who fought down south are crazy. They don't know anything about fighting Indians." The Army was paying Bridger $10 a day for his expertise. Not even Carrington, the fort commander, was paid as much.

Col. Carrington decided that from that day on, they must use extreme caution when riding to the relief of the wood train. And on the 19th of December, when the wood train came under attack again, Carrington ordered Capt. James W. Powell out with instructions not to pursue the Indians across Lodge Trail Ridge.

The cautious Powell followed his orders to the letter and returned safely, his command intact, the wood train safe. But while a few praised Carrington for this good sense, others were speaking against him, criticizing him for not carrying the fight to the Indians.

Capt. Fetterman, one of his biggest critics, boasted, "A single company of regulars could whip a thousand Indians." After some more thought, he added, "A full regiment could whip the entire array of hostile tribes."

A short time later, Fetterman swore, "With eighty men I could ride through the Sioux nation."

And then on December 21, Capt. William J. Fetterman got his chance. That morning, the buglar called *Reveille*, Sick Call and Guard Mounting and the day was begun. In a while, the wood train moved out with a 90-man guard. No sooner had they cleared the gate than the picket on Pilot Hill began signaling: Indians!

Col. Carrington's first thought was to send Capt. Powell to the relief of the wood train. Powell had done well, followed his orders to the letter, on December 19. But now, standing in front of headquarters was Company A and Capt. Fetterman. Fetterman reminded Carrington that he outranked Powell and insisted firmly that he be allowed to go after the Indians.

Carrington approved, but ordered, "Support the wood train. Relieve it and report to me. Do not engage or pursue Indians at its expense. Under no circumstances pursue over the ridge, that is, Lodge Trail Ridge."

Fetterman saluted, spun on his heel and ordered his command into action. In just minutes, he would disobey orders, lead his entire command into eternity, and march into American history books.

Capt. Frederick H. Brown, recently promoted and ready to return east, was eager for another crack at the Indians, and Lt. Grummond asked to lead the deceased Bingham's cavalry. In addition to these three officers, two scouts from the quartermaster division volunteered to ride out. They were James Wheatley and Isaac Fisher. Both were ex-Civil War officers and both were armed with repeating Henry rifles. The total force would number 81, the exact number that Fetterman claimed that he needed to "ride through the entire Sioux nation."

Fetterman took Company A and a detachment from C Company out the gate on the double. Instead of heading for the wagons, he used the same trail Carrington had used on December 6, the north trail around the Sullivant Hills.

Frances Grummond heard her husband's orders: "Report to Captain Fetterman, implicitly obey orders, and never leave."

She went into her house and closed the door. She dreaded the wait, but within a few minutes, other women came to stay with her. Together, they waited for the return of the soldiers, unwilling to speak about the possibility that some might not return. It was nearing 11:30 a.m. when Lt. Grummond's 27-man cavalry command marched through the open gates, on their way to catch up with and support Fetterman's infantrymen.

Moments later, several Indians showed themselves along Piney Creek in front of the fort, and Col. Carrington ordered that a round from the howitzer be fired. A spherical case-shot was touched off and landed close enough to the Indians that they scampered out of sight.

Col. Carrington sent Assistant Surgeon C.M. Hines to the wood train just in case there might be injuries. At the wood train minutes later, Surgeon Hines found that the wagon was not under attack, so he turned around the north end of the Sullivant Hills to intercept Fetterman's command. But all Hines saw there were hundreds of Indians swarming about Lodge Trail Ridge. He saw nothing of Fetterman or his men.

Immediately, Surgeon Hines rode to the fort, reporting that he could not find Fetterman. At first, there was little concern, since those in the fort figured Fetterman was retreating to safety by one of the roads and would soon come into sight of the fort.

Then, just moments later, shots were fired northwest of the fort. Col. Carrington sounded a general alarm and ordered Capt. Ten Eyck out with infantrymen, a supply wagon, and mounted men to guard it, about 54 men in all.

A few more shots were heard in the distance, then the gunfire grew more rapid. There was a desperate fight going on. There was no doubt about that. The shooting was coming from the valley beyond Lodge Trail Ridge.

Frances Grummond remembered, "Then followed a few quick volleys, then scattering volleys, and then dead silence."

Col. Carrington reassured the women, but when Ten Eyck got to a hill overlooking the valley where Fetterman had ridden, he sent back Carrington's orderly, Archibald Sample, with a message.

Sample lashed his horse back to the fort, carrying a written message from Ten Eyck. The valley, according to the note, was full of Indians and there was no sign of Fetterman. Fear swept the women.

Carrington sent another 40 men to assist Ten Eyck. With them went an ambulance and 3,000 rounds of ammunition. Ten Eyck's orders were: "Unite with Fetterman, fire slowly, and keep men in hand."

Then Col. Carrington turned to the task of protecting the fort. Fifty-five men, plus teamsters, were out with the wood train. Fetterman's unit numbered 81 men, and Ten Eyck's command had 94. Seven men lay disabled in the hospital. With prisoners from the guardhouse, civilians, and quartermaster employees, Col. Carrington could muster only 119.

While this was going on, the women and children were terror stricken. Visions of all sorts of atrocities were with them every moment. The end might come for them at any time. Surely the Indians would over-run the fort and kill them all. There was little hope for survival. Fear had swept the fort. And worst of all, there was nothing to do but wait.

The sunset gun fired and night came, but there was still no relief. Where were the soldiers? Were they all dead? Would the Indians kill them all, the women and children included?

All the women huddled inside Mrs. Wands' cabin. There they remained, fearing the worst. It was near dark when the wagons from Ten Eyck's command returned to the fort. The women cringed at this sound. They knew now that they would soon learn the horrible truth. The gates swung open, and the wagons rolled solemnly over the frozen ground. All the observers could see were misshapened arms and legs sticking out of the wagons.

They knew now that the worst had happened. The wagons hauled in 49 mutilated bodies and took them directly to the hospital. Someone told the women, "No more were to come in."

It was left to Margaret Carrington to tell Frances Grummond that her husband was not found. Mrs. Carrington then took her into her home that night, trying to comfort her. Outside, the wind howled, and sleet and snow lashed at the fort. The temperature was on its way to a below-zero reading. Inside, Frances Grummond wondered what had happened to her husband. Was he still alive and being tortured? Or was he dead?

That night, Col. Carrington drafted two messages to be carried to Fort Laramie by a volunteer, John (Portugee) Phillips. One message was for Gen. Philip St. George Cooke, the commander of the Department of the Platte. The other was for Gen. U.S. Grant in Washington. Carrington wrote of the massacre and asked for reinforcements. He requested the arms promised, the new Spencer rifles that had been sent from Fort Leavenworth in mid-September but had not arrived. He asked that he be sent either cavalry or infantry, two companies of cavalry or four of infantry.

Before Phillips rode out, he visited Frances Grummond. Phillips, born in the Azores, spoke only broken English, but he told her, "I will go if it costs me my life. I am going for your sake." (Phillips rode the 236 miles in four days and delivered the messages.)

Most felt their lives depended on Phillips. He was riding for help. Col. Carrington and the others feared an attack on the stockade. Windows were boarded up and doors barred. Without making it generally known, emergency plans were made to move the ten women at the fort into the magazine. When the Indians attacked and all appeared lost, an officer would blow up the magazine, killing the women and children in one gigantic explosion.

Snow continued to fall, and as it blew and drifted against the walls of the fort, a new threat piled up with it. The snow was forming a huge ramp against the walls, one that the Indians could run up and easily drop over the wall and down into the fort. Col. Carrington assigned men to try to keep the drifts shoveled away from the wall.

By nine o'clock that night, the temperature had dropped to 30 degrees below zero. Those on guard duty feared another kind of death now. At those temperatures and with the wind so intense, they would surely freeze to death before the Indians could kill them. Several suffered frostbite, even when the tour of duty at each guard post was limited to 20 minutes.

After a restless night, Col. Carrington greeted the gray, cold dawn. He had not slept but did not yet feel the inevitable exhaustion. Studying the sky, he decided the clouds forecast heavy snow. (They were in for a blizzard that lasted several days.) Carrington considered the risk from the Indians and the weather and gave orders to ride out and find the rest of his men. He said, "I will not let the Indians entertain the conviction that the dead cannot and will not be rescued."

To Frances Grummond, Carrington promised, "I will bring back to you your husband."

Scout Jim Bridger rode out first and set pickets at high points along their route to the battlefield. Carrington, Capt. Ten Eyck, Lt. Winfield Scott Matson, a surgeon named Ould and 80 heavily-clad men rode out to search for the bodies. The temperature remained near zero throughout the day.

As they drew nearer the battlesite, the mules pulling the wagons became skittish and hard to control. The mules could smell the blood-soaked ground, and on the wind-whipped site, it was all the soldiers could do to keep them under control. The frozen, naked bodies of the dead soldiers lay among the boulders on the high side of the road. The gray, cold bodies were horribly mutilated.

Lt. Grummond was found along the road down toward Peno Creek. His fingers were chopped off, his body filled with arrows and his head nearly severed.

The two civilians, Wheatley and Fisher, had taken a heavy toll of the Indians. Spent cartridges and frozen pools of blood surrounded them. Wheatley had 105 arrows in his body.

Near dark, the somber detail returned to the fort and unloaded the frozen, grotesque bodies in the guard house, turning it into what one private called "a death house." Col. Carrington went to Frances Grummond's room and gave her an envelope with a lock of her husband's hair.

Frances Grummond lost her husband to Indians at Fort Phil Kearny.
(Author's Collection)

In the hours and days that followed, the widowed Frances Grummond suffered the sounds of carpenters building coffins and somber men digging a burial trench in the stone-cold ground. The trench was 50 feet long and 7 feet deep and 7 feet wide. The pine coffins were built in the headquarters building, where Frances lived with the Carringtons. During these terrible days, she often wondered about a picture of her that her husband carried, "What Indian Chief had it now?"

Two enlisted men were fitted into each coffin. The three officers had individual coffins. On December 25, the coffins were lined up, the plan being to bury the dead on that day. But the trench diggers were not ready. The frozen ground slowed the diggers. The snow continued, and the inhabitants of the lonely fort continued to fear an Indian attack. Finally, on December 26, the dead were buried. There were, however, no ceremonies or military honors due to the real threat of Indians. (In October 1888, the Fetterman Massacre bodies, plus 37 others killed at or near Fort Phil Kearny, were moved to the National Cemetery at the Custer Battlefield.)

The first relief following the Fetterman disaster came the next day, December 27, when Capt. George B. Dandy, Lieutenants Thomas J. Gregg and Alphonse Borsman and 22 enlisted men broke through the snow and into the fort. These men had braved the storm and marched up from Fort Reno. And there was more relief on January 16, 1867, when Lt. Col. Henry Walton Wessells arrived with four infantry companies and two cavalry companies. Wessells was there to replace Carrington. In the mail Wessells brought, Carrington found he had been reassigned to the command of Fort Casper, the new headquarters for the 18th U.S. Infantry Regiment.

A letter for Frances from her sister, Florence Crochnour, revealed that the sister had been having premonitions of Indian trouble. Frances Grummond suffered similar premonitions still. At night, she dreamed of Indian attacks. She wanted to leave this place and began planning to return to the East.

She could no longer live at the fort since her husband was no longer in the Army. That was the Army way. So she sold her furniture, and at 1:30 p.m. on January 23, 1867, Frances Grummond rode out of Fort Phil Kearny headed toward Fort Reno.

The trip in the middle of winter was grueling, but the Army made the best preparation possible. She described the wagon in which she rode: "The wagon covers of cloth were first doubled, and both sides and ends of the wagon bodies were boarded up, with a window in each end. A door at the back of each wagon swung on hinges ... and near the door was a small sheet iron stove made from stove-pipe, with a carefully adjusted smoke escape through the wagon-cover above."

Frances had pine knots and blocks of wood on board for fuel. She was in the advanced stages of pregnancy, and travel in the cold and over the frozen, snow-clogged trail was uncomfortable to say the least. For a bed, she rested on a mattress of straw covered by a hospital mattress. Over that was spread a buffalo robe given her by Margaret Carrington. And she had a wolf robe given her by Portugee Phillips. She called her wagon a "traveling house."

In one of the other wagons rode the body of her husband. The pine box had been disinterred so she could return him to Tennessee.

Forty infantrymen and 20 cavalrymen escorted the wagon train on the first day of the trip to Fort Reno, near present Sussex in Johnson County. Travel was slow due to the cold and snow. Men went in advance to dig out the deepest snow drifts. The wagons made only six miles in eight hours. Their camp that night was on a hill to protect against Indians. The cold and wind were nearly unbearable.

The legs of one of the wagon drivers froze from the knees down and were amputated when they reached Fort Reno. The thermometer in the headquarters wagon congealed, but not before it reached 40 degrees below zero their second day on the trail. The wary mules kept breaking out of their harness and running off. Often, the going was precarious, with the wagons tottering recklessly or bumping over rough, frozen paths. Several times, Frances Grummond said that she "clung for dear life to the sides of the wagon, with eyes shut and jaws clamped."

From time to time, there were Indian alarms, but often they turned out to be distant buffalo herds. The wagons finally plowed through the 65 miles to Fort Reno in just three days after leaving Fort Phil Kearny. Three days later, they started out again, this time headed for Fort Casper. Indians near Fort Casper appeared, but ran off and caused them no trouble.

At Fort Casper, Col. Carrington's orders had been changed. Washington had decided the 18th Infantry would be headquartered at Fort McPherson, not at Fort Casper. So the colonel and the others began again. The wagons continued their trek toward Bridger's Ferry. Frances Grummond's brother, William Wirt Courtney, from Tennessee, met her there. He helped his sister the rest of the way and by late February 1867, they had arrived at Fort McPherson, where they boarded the Union Pacific Railroad for the ride home.

The entire trip, from Fort Phil Kearny, Wyoming Territory, to Franklin, Tennessee, took seven weeks. Frances, her dead husband and her brother arrived in Tennessee in March.

Lt. George W. Grummond was buried at Franklin, Tennessee in Rest Haven Cemetery. His plain, granite slab noted that he: "Died at Fort Kearny, Wyo. December 22, 1866."

Not long after, Frances delivered George Grummond's son, William Wands Grummond. (The name "Wands" was apparently for her good friends at Fort Phil Kearny, Lt. and Mrs. Alexander H. Wands and their small son, Bobby.)

A few years later, while visiting a sister in Cincinnati, Frances Grummond learned of the death of Margaret Carrington. She sent her regrets to Col. Carrington, and the correspondence that ensued led to the marriage of Frances and Col. Carrington, then a Professor of Military Science at Wabash College in Crawfordsville, Indiana. That was in 1871.

Carrington had retired from the Army in 1870. Besides his job at Wabash College, he also was a treaty negotiator with the Flathead Indians in Montana and authored five history books. Carrington died on October 26, 1912.

The Carringtons had returned to Wyoming during July, 1908, to help dedicate a monument on the site of the Fetterman Fight. The monument still stands today. The inscription is as follows:

"ON THIS FIELD ON THE 21ST OF
DECEMBER, 1866,
THREE COMMISSIONED OFFICERS AND
SEVENTY SIX PRIVATES
OF THE 18TH U.S. INFANTRY, AND OF THE
2ND U.S. CAVALRY AND FOUR CIVILIANS
UNDER THE COMMAND OF CAPTAIN BREVET-
LIEUTENANT COLONEL WILLIAM J. FETTERMAN

WERE KILLED BY AN OVERWHELMING
FORCE OF SIOUX UNDER THE COMMAND OF
RED CLOUD.
THERE WERE NO SURVIVORS.

A couple of years later, Frances Grummond Carrington wrote and published her book, *My Army Life*. She died at Hyde Park, Massachusetts in 1911.

Aftermath: Following the winter of 1866-67, the Army remained at Fort Phil Kearny. That summer, during August, there was another incident. Again it started with an attack on woodcutters. A company of the 27th Infantry and four civilians worked at a site about two miles south of present Story along what is now called "Wagon Box Fight County Road." Indians attacked. Captain James W. Powell quickly commanded that the wagon boxes be turned up on their sides for fortification. His men were by now armed with the new Allen modification of the Springfield breech-loading rifles and their hail of lead held off a four-and-one-half-hour attack. A force from the fort finally rescued them but not before they had killed an estimated 60 Indians and wounded another 120. Powell's losses were six killed and two wounded. A flag and a stone monument mark that site today.

The United States government had seen enough and called for a meeting with the Indians that led to the Treaty of Laramie of 1868. Fort Phil Kearny and the other forts were closed, the Bozeman Trail was closed, and whites promised again that they would stay out of the area, a promise they kept for less than a decade.

6

Frances Roe:
A Love Story

The tired woman sat staring at her patiently written manuscript. She planned to share her story, her story of life in the 1800s. And her story was different, for it was a story of frontier living, of hardships wrought by a desire to be with the man she loved.

She looked around the room in the quiet, tidy home in Port Orange, Florida, remembering the handsome lieutenant, her husband, dressed in his light-blue overcoat and big campaign hat with the brim turned up. Now, as he sat across the room from her, he was no longer that dashing young Infantry officer, but a man nearing 60 and tormented by chronic gastritis and severe headaches. He was a man who had longed to achieve the rank of major in an Army that kept him a second lieutenant for a dozen years. Still, he was the man she loved, the man she adored as much now as nearly 40 years ago when she became Mrs. Fayette Washington Roe.

Frances Roe had carefully collected letters written decades earlier, and now they were prepared and off to a publisher, D. Appleton and Company. Like her life, the manuscript was dedicated: "To My Comrade Faye."

Frances Marie Antoinette Mack of Orleans, Jefferson County, New York was the daughter of Ralph Gilbert Mack and the former Mary Coulton. She was schooled at Elmira, New York, and it was there that she met a young West Virginian, Fayette Washington Roe.

Young Mr. Roe was the son of Naval Commander Francis Asbury Roe. He had attended school at the Brooklyn Polytechnic Institute and Burlington College before entering the United States Military Academy at West Point in the summer of 1867.

On June 12, 1871, Cadet Roe became 2nd Lieutenant Roe, graduating 40th in a class of 41, and in August, he and Frances were married. Almost immediately, he was posted to Fort Lyon, Colorado Territory to join the Third Infantry Regiment.

Fort Lyon, located in southeast Colorado near where the Purgatorie River joins the Arkansas, was near the site of Bent's Fort. Fort Lyon protected the Santa Fe Trail, as did Forts Zarah, Larned and Dodge.

Their route west took them through central Kansas, past Cheyenne Wells, Colorado Territory, and into the scruffy little town of Kit Carson. Frances' first look at the little town did not leave her impressed. She claimed that in the moonlight, Kit Carson's buildings looked like chunks of clay. The hotel was made of dirt with dirt floors, according to her, and she was sure that in the houses one might find "spooks and creepy things." As to the people: "Not one woman have I seen here, but there are men—any number of dreadful-looking men—each one armed with big pistols, and leather belts full of cartridges."

She was glad to leave the next morning by stage for Fort Lyon, and she asked and received permission to ride up top with the driver. He told her about the hardships of stage driving, especially mentioning the sandstorms he had endured. It was a 50-mile trip on the "jerkey," the name they all gave the stagecoach. She wrote, "It seesawed back and forth and then sideways, in an awful breakneck way."

And so, Lt. Roe and Frances settled into Fort Lyon in October 1871. The fort's buildings were of clay and mud, mixed. They were low and broad with thick walls. All the windows were heavily shuttered to keep the sand out during the frequent sandstorms the stage driver had told her about. A small ditch around the fort brought water for the trees and lawns, but water for the houses was hauled by wagon from the Arkansas River and kept in barrels.

Her first morning on the post began with cannons blasting and her house shaking. Drums were rolling and a fife playing, and dogs began howling and barking. She awoke with a start at all this, fearing the worst. It had to be Indians! They were attacking!

From out of the black came the mournful notes of three or four buglers. She could hear men shouting. Certainly she was in danger! She got out of bed, tripped across the room to a window and peered out into the darkness.

Her husband, still in bed, slept on. Then she called to him. Half asleep, he told her that it was only reveille. So began Frances Roe's life of excitement on a military post.

It wasn't long until she saw her first Indians. She wrote that they were "painted, dirty, and nauseous-smelling savages!" And just a few days later, on a trip to nearby Las Animas, she had her second experience.

Frances and the wives of two other officers rode to Las Animas in an Army ambulance pulled by four "shaved-tail" mules. These mules were coal-black except for their noses. The driver, the best on the post, delivered the ladies to the small stores in the half-Mexican town, and they began going over the goods.

In one store, while they looked over the merchandise in the narrow aisles, there was a sudden commotion in the street outside. Almost instantly, 10 or 12 Ute Indian men reined their ponies to a halt and slid to the ground right in front of the store. Frances said she noticed the smell right away when they came through the door. Their faces were streaked red and green, she remembered later, and their hair "was roped with strips of bright-colored stuff, and hung down on each side of their shoulders in front, and on the crown of each black head was a small, tightly plaited lock, ornamented at the top with a feather, a piece of tin, or something fantastic." Each wore "dirty old shirts" with a blanket over that. Their moccasins and trousers were made of skin.

She looked toward the door, but another Ute had filled the door with his piebald pony, the front hooves on the sill, the head and shoulders blocking the door. Frances feared they would all be murdered!

The Utes pushed their way by the women and went directly to the store's counter. There, they demanded powder, balls and percussion caps for their old rifles. Outside, other Utes waited on their ponies as those inside jabbered at the clerk. He was nodding and giving them everything they asked for, but Frances Roe noticed that his face was "greenish white" all through the transactions.

She knew the Utes had been on the warpath only two years before. It was apparent to her that they were readying themselves to renew those times.

And then, just as suddenly as they came storming into the store, they shoved the women aside and retreated to their waiting ponies. In a cloud of dust and amid wild screams, they thundered down the dusty street and out of the little town, headed to the river.

The storekeeper, trying to save face, said they were only after ammunition to go after some Cheyennes that camped nearby. The Utes and Cheyennes were bitter enemies, he said, and he could see the Utes were much frightened.

Mrs. Roe could only remember the "greenish-white" face of the storeclerk. He was the one who was frightened—along with her and the other women, of course. She heard later that the Utes had indeed attacked the Cheyenne camp, killing two or three of their dreaded enemies.

And there was excitement of other kinds, too. That afternoon, after finishing their shopping, the women headed back to the fort, the four matched mules pulling the ambulance. On the way, the mules became skittish and broke into a run, dragging the swaying ambulance all the way to the fort. With the women hanging on for dear life, they charged into the fort and straight to the corral where they came to a sudden stop. The driver was embarrassed and aggravated at the mules. Mrs. Roe wrote later, "One leader looked around at us and commenced to bray, but the driver was in no mood for such insolence, and jerked the poor thing almost down."

Throughout her stay in the West, Frances loved to hunt and fish. She learned to ride the army way—"tight in the saddle"— very early and was often off riding one of her many horses. She wrote with pride, years later, that she had ridden 22 horses that no woman had ever ridden before. She learned to jump cavalry hurdles and ditches and hunted rabbits and coyotes with greyhounds.

She could shoot the short, cavalry rifle, the Spencer, and could hit a four-inch bull's-eye at 75 paces. She learned to fire a pistol from the saddle, and she also shot a Springfield infantry rifle but complained that it almost made her deaf and "rudely kicked her over on her back." She said of the bullet she fired from the Springfield, "I expect that ball is still on its way to Mars or perhaps the moon. This earth it certainly did not hit!"

Her first buffalo hunt was in November 1871. Besides her husband, two lieutenants rode out 15 or 16 miles from the post to a herd. She did not kill any of the great beasts, but the others killed four. The carcasses were returned to the post and skinned. They took the hides to an Indian camp to be tanned.

Antelope were plentiful, too, but it was dangerous to run them since prairie dog towns were dangerous for the horses. If one used hounds, they invariably returned with their feet full of cactus spines. She wrote of how hunters tied a red handkerchief on a rifle and placed it on a hill. The wary, shy, little antelope, their curiosity up, would then walk toward the red, flapping handkerchief. It was a slow process, she pointed out, but then antelope meat was a pleasant break from the beef that they ate all the time.

Christmas services were held in a little chapel at Fort Lyon. An Infantry sergeant played the organ, and Frances and others sang in a little choir. Faye gave her a saddle for Christmas.

The enlisted men got their customary plum cakes, rich with fruit and sugar and baked by the officers' wives. And there were buffalo, antelope, boiled ham, vegetables, pies, cakes, pickles, dried "apple-

Charming, brave Frances Roe with one of her favorite hounds.
(Author's Collection)

duff" and coffee. Later in the week, Frances attended a dance and she recalled wearing a "nile-green silk" dress that she said "showed off my splendid coat of tan only too well."

Frances Roe experienced her first serious sandstorm in January, shortly after the 1872 new year. She was out riding with two lieutenants from the fort when the storm came up. They made a dash for the fort, arriving about the same time as the storm. It was Monday and most of the women lost their laundry. The wind was as strong as a hurricane, Frances exaggerated.

And then Lt. and Mrs. Roe were ordered to Camp Supply in Oklahoma Territory about 250 miles southeast of Fort Lyon. They had feared this all along. Their information warned them of the worst. The post, they had heard, had log houses and was built in the hot sand hills. The dusty, hot post was surrounded by Indians.

The Roes were allowed to only take part of their belongings, a half-wagon full. It was distressing to Frances, and she was miserable. There had even been talk that she would have to leave her greyhound puppy, Hal, behind. Finally, she resolved, "I have cried and cried over all these things until I am simply hideous, but I have to go just the same, and I have made up my mind never again to make myself so wholly disagreeable about a move, no matter where we may have to go."

Then she recalled something her grandmother once told her: "It is a dreadful thing not to become a woman when one ceases to be a girl!" It was time for Frances Roe to become a woman. She seldom complained about her lot in life after that.

Hal, the puppy, went along, and by May 1872, they were at Camp Supply. At this place, there were three units of cavalry and three companies of the Third Infantry. Two of the cavalry units were black. She noted that the Indians called them buffalo soldiers because their hair was like that of the "matted cushion that is between the horns of the buffalo."

As far as Indians were concerned, she wrote that there were Comanches, Apaches, Kiowas, Cheyennes and friendly Arapahoes surrounding the post. And on one of her first times riding, she encountered a lone Indian rider. She and two other civilians were riding down a road next to a field of wild sunflowers when the lone Indian appeared.

They turned back toward Camp Supply, finally reaching the sutler's store just as the Indian overtook them. The lone Indian circled them twice, yelled, "How!" and charged off down the sunflower road as fast as he had come up it. The next morning, a soldier was shot and killed less than a quarter of a mile from the camp while chasing a strayed mule. Frances became more cautious after those incidents.

Later in the summer, 40 or 50 Indians charged into the camp, rode to the garden and completely destroyed the melons. By the time an infantry company came on the scene, the damage was done. And when the cavalry arrived, the Indians rode off toward the hills without opposition. This occurred about two weeks after couriers from Fort Dodge to Camp Supply were found dead, shot in the back. It was a strange relationship the Army had with the Indians.

Frances Roe complained about the disagreeable way the Indians came to her windows. "Sometimes," she wrote, "before you have heard a sound you will be conscious of an uncomfortable feeling, and looking around you will discover five or six Indians, large and small, peering at you through the windows, each ugly nose pressed flat against the glass! It is enough to drive one mad."

Camp Supply officers' quarters were as bad as they suspected. They were made of vertical cottonwood logs with the bark still on. The roofs were of poles and mud. Some rooms had sand floors. Despite all the trouble with Indians, she wrote, "The army of bugs that hide underneath the bark during the day and march upon us at night is to be dreaded about as much as a whole tribe of Indians."

The "whole tribe of Indians" finally attacked one morning in October. It was about 1 a.m. when the attack came on the corner of the fortifications where the officers' quarters were located. Frances Roe, armed with a pistol, and an officer's wife from next door, put on waterproof coats over their gowns and sat on the steps of the Roe quarters. They sat there until dawn, fearfully awaiting the Indians to overrun the fort. The threat passed. In the final analysis, it was decided the Indians were trying to divert the Army's attention long enough to steal the cavalry horses at the other end of the compound. Their plan failed this time.

The year 1873, the Roes' second full year on the American Frontier, proved to be as varied as the previous year. Frances saw the harshness of military life for women when a captain named White died at Camp Supply. His wife, with a small baby and four other children, began making preparations to return north to live with relatives. She had to leave her quarters as soon as the baby could travel. The women on the post sewed, making as many clothes for her and the children as possible before she began the 150 miles or so to the railroad. Her husband was buried at Camp Supply. There was no chaplain to speak over his January funeral.

That same month, the Army was faced with a new problem. Whiskey was being smuggled to Camp Supply inside bags of oats. The camp was becoming a haven for whiskey runners, most of whom lived between there and Fort Dodge. The Indian women in the area complained to the sutler since it was their men who were paying high prices for the illegal whiskey. (The Indians often traded buffalo robes for the whiskey.)

The Army decided the place to stop this activity was at a mail station called the Cimarron Redoubt. The post was located about 40 miles from Camp Supply and Fort Dodge. Relay mules were kept there for the mail wagon and escort running weekly between Fort Dodge and Camp Supply. Normally, there was a sergeant and privates stationed at the post. This whiskey problem, the Army decided, called for an officer to be assigned to the outpost, as well.

A lieutenant was sent to the post, but he became ill, and Lt. Roe was sent to replace him. Mrs. Roe insisted that she be allowed to accompany her husband.

Permission was granted, and on arrival, Frances Roe went to work to make the quarters as homey as possible. The walls of their living quarters were made of sandbags. She staked grain sacks to the floor, then covered them with rugs she had brought. Turkey-red curtains dressed up the one small window. The Roes lived there for five weeks, 40 miles from the nearest military post.

The highlight of the stay was a visit from an Arapahoe chief named Powder-Face and his beautiful, slim young wife, Wauk. Following the visit, an Arapahoe named Dog brought her a gift from the chief, a strawberry roan that she named Powder-Face.

In addition to increasing the manpower at the Cimarron Redoubt, the Army sent out a cavalry unit to visit whiskey ranches at Bluff Creek and to chase down other leads about the illegal dealers. Over the weeks that the Roes were at the redoubt, the Army managed to make several arrests and destroy hundreds of gallons of whiskey.

They were back at Camp Supply before February ended but soon received orders to move back to Fort Lyon in early summer. The trip north to Dodge City took three days. It was slower than usual because they encountered an enormous buffalo herd that blocked their way. In addition, they had a broken wagon. The first night out was especially bad because they did not make Cimarron Redoubt, the halfway point. Instead, they had to camp in a coulee, and Hal, the greyhound, "acted like a crazy dog— barking and growling."

It was a restless night, but the fear of Indians passed, and they were up and rolling early the next morning. The red curtains still hung in the redoubt as they passed, and they reached Fort Dodge after another day of travel. They planned on catching a train, but they also awaited the arrival of a servant girl from Kansas City. They decided to take a hotel room in nearby Dodge City while they waited.

The stay in Dodge City was not a good one. Their trouble began when Lt. and Mrs. Roe started out of the hotel to take Hal, the dog, for a walk. The hotel owner warned that they had better not. At least, he warned, put the dog on a leash.

Lt. Roe said he would have anyone arrested who tried to take the dog.

That would never work, the owner told them, unless they wanted to argue with two or more revolvers. Besides, he added, there was no one to make arrests. And if the thief couldn't have the dog, he would probably shoot him anyway.

The second night, Lt. and Mrs. Roe settled into their second-story hotel room, the window open to let in the cool night air. Hal, who had been sleeping in the corner of the room, suddenly let out a low growl. Then there were shots, some striking the hotel building, and people talking loudly and running. Someone screamed, "I'm shot! I'm shot!" And then they heard a body fall to the ground beneath their second-story hotel window.

The wounded man was not dead yet. He pleaded with the shooters. Someone shot him again. He called out, "Oh, my lassie, my poor lassie!"

Frances Roe wrote later that they had to "listen to the moans and death gurgle of that murdered man."

This event lasted for perhaps five or 10 minutes. At the first shot, someone had called out, "Vigilante! Vigilante!" But the vigilantes did not arrive until after the man was dead and the murderers had fled.

The next morning, the hotel owner and others learned what had happened. A black man living in town had hired out to take three or four men to Fort Dodge in his wagon. Fort Dodge lay five miles east of town, and on the way, he realized they were up to no good and returned them to Dodge. They took offense and he ran to the house of other blacks across from the hotel. The men in the wagon commenced shooting wildly, killing one of the black man's mules. The black man was hit, too. He left a trail of blood that crossed the street.

The hotel owner told the Roes that to go into the street would have meant certain death. Mrs. Roe concluded that Dodge City was "dreadful and has the reputation of being one of the very worst in the West since the railroad has been built."

Their train left Dodge City for Granada, Colorado Territory, a short time later and took them to within 40 or 50 miles of Fort Lyon, where they were met by an ambulance that took them the rest of the way.

The maid from Kansas City had arrived and traveled with them, but she was emaciated with tuberculosis and soon had to return home. Sometime late that summer, Mrs. Roe returned east for a visit. And when she returned in October, it was to find that during the previous hours someone had tried to kill her husband.

This had occurred while Lt. Roe waited in Granada for Frances' train to arrive. Roe and the quartermaster's clerk had gone for an evening stroll. Granada's gambling places and saloons were busy, their kerosene lamps splashing light onto the dark, dirty street. Suddenly, a voice called from a dark passageway, "You are the man I want!"

Out of the dark a man jumped, so close that when he aimed the pistol, he struck Lt. Roe in the face. An instant before it exploded, Roe ducked out of the way. The blood from the wound where the barrel struck him quickly filled his left eye. The bullet must have missed.

At the same instant, Roe went under his coat for one of his pistols. The clerk with him now ran away as the shooter came out of the alley and ran in the other direction, stopping only to fire wildly at Roe. Roe returned the fire at this stranger. His shots were returned until both men's guns were empty. And when it was quiet in the street again, Roe realized he had been hit in the ankle.

When Mrs. Roe's train arrived, Roe and his escort took all precautions to get out of town without more shooting. Lt. Roe had already found out that the man who did the shooting was Billy Oliver, a horse thief who had spent some time in the jail at Fort Lyon the previous summer.

Oliver was arrested not long after and placed in the cellar of the jail at Las Animas. There, he was chained to a post. He claimed he'd kill the jailer the first day he was out and Lt. Roe the next. His trial was set for May 1874.

The Territorial Court met, found Oliver guilty and sentenced him to 10 years in the penitentiary at Canon City. And it was about the same time that the Roes received word that they were moving again. This time, their destination was Holly Springs, Mississippi in the Department of the Gulf.

The stay in the East would last until the late summer of 1877. During that time, Lt. Faye Roe's company would make 21 moves. He and Frances lived in Baton Rouge and New Orleans, Louisiana for a while. They were at Vicksburg, where they stayed with former Confederate President Jefferson Davis' niece and met and dined with Davis on one occasion.

In September, 1877, they were in Pittsburgh, Pennsylvania awaiting orders and a train west to Montana Territory. President Rutherford Hayes had sent part of the Third Infantry to Pittsburgh to deal with the great coal strike, an outgrowth of the railway strikes that swept the nation that year. Matters worsened for the Third Infantry when Congress went home without passing an appropriation bill. For three months, the officers and men went without pay. Mrs. Roe wondered what Congress would say if the Army, as a body, said, "We are tired, Uncle, dear, and are going home for the summer to rest. You will have to get along without us and manage the Indians and strikers the best way you can."

Not long after, a special train left Pittsburgh with the Third Infantry aboard. A week later, they arrived in Corinne, Utah Territory and set up a tent city where they would live until the wagons were ready to travel north to Montana.

For the march north, Frances Roe loaded into a wagon with a knock-down bed, two little stoves, a mess-chest and bedding wrapped tightly in canvas. They began each day at four o'clock, had breakfast by five and were moving by six. They traveled six to eight hours a day.

She was sick part of the time, and Lt. Roe walked along-side the wagon as much as he could. The wagons did not travel as fast as the marching soldiers, but when they took their 10-minute break each hour, the wagons caught up.

It was during this trip that she wrote of the role of the Army wives. "We know," she began, "if the world does not, that the part we are to take on this march is most important. We will see that the tents are made comfortable and cheerful at every camp; that the little dinner after the weary march, the early breakfast, and the cold luncheon are each and all as dainty as camp cooking will permit. Yes, we are sometimes called 'camp followers,' but we do not mind— it probably originated with some envious old bachelor officer."

A blizzard at Ryan's Junction, Idaho Territory, slowed the Army's advance in October, but by November they had arrived at Camp Baker, Montana Territory. The camp was nearly isolated. Supplies had to be hauled in by ox train. The camp was 500 miles from a railroad. And the trip to the camp had been a harrowing trip over steep grades, across the Missouri River at Confederate Gulch aboard a flatboat ferry, and into the Belt Mountains. But the reward for the weary travelers was beautiful scenery that included snowcapped mountains.

For Frances Roe, however, the most memorable thing about Camp Baker was the loss of her beloved greyhound, Hal. The dog was hunting with Lt. Roe when he collapsed and died. A detail was sent out to bury the dog, with orders to cover the grave with glass to keep the wolves out of the grave. The men later put up a board monument at the site.

On two days notice, Lt. Roe's company was ordered to Helena and then north into Indian country. Frances did not accompany him beyond Helena, but roomed at the National (or International) and Cosmopolitan Hotels that summer. Late in the summer, during an outbreak of typhoid fever, she caught a stage north to join her husband. This stage ride was one of her worst. She wrote that this stagecoach was the "bob-back-and-forth kind that pitches you off the seat every five minutes."

She continued, noting that the first two or three times, a smile and apology was sufficient, but "after a while your hat will not stay in place and your head becomes sensitive." After a while, she added, "You discover that the passenger is the most disagreeable person you ever saw, and that the man sitting beside you is inconsiderate and selfish, and really occupying two thirds of the seat."

She asked to ride up top, but the driver would not hear of it. Every 20 miles, for a total of 140 miles, they changed teams, and the road was so narrow in spots they had to unload and lift the stage out of the path into the rocks so that ox trains could creep past them. She said the stage "was swaying like a living thing."

Frances Roe was the only woman on the stage, and the driver and three male passengers were constantly telling her what to do. She concluded, "It was bad enough to have to obey just one man, when at home, and then to have four strange men—three of them idiots, too—suddenly take upon themselves to order me around was not to be endured."

Finally, after the stage changed drivers at a way station, she asked again if she could ride up top. The driver granted permission, and she wrote, "I had peace and fresh air—the glorious air of Montana." Her husband Faye met her at Fort Benton with an ambulance, and they got underway to Fort Shaw, about 20 miles west of present Great Falls.

The Roes lived at Fort Shaw over a year and then were transferred to Fort Ellis. Then, in June, 1880, Faye was transferred back to Fort Shaw because he was the senior second lieutenant in the Third Infantry Regiment and was assigned to become the commander of C Company.

Six weeks later, Lt. Roe's company was ordered to Fort Maginnis, less than 20 miles northeast of present Lewiston. The Army ordered them there to build new log quarters.

This was a 150-mile trip. There were 50 men in the command. It was a rough trip. In one spot, it took 12 mules to pull the wagons up the hill. At one point they were warned of horse thieves in the area and managed to slip through without the loss of one animal.

As far as Frances was concerned, the sun was her biggest problem. She wore an officer's white cork helmet, but that didn't seem to keep her from getting too much sun. And when her face began to peel, she claimed that she looked like "a zebra or an Indian with war paint on."

Roe's command arrived at Fort Maginnis in August. Cree Indians from Canada were in the area to hunt and had their villages set up. Their tipis dappled the green of the valley. There was plenty of game. Deer, grouse, and prairie chickens were in abundance.

Lt. Roe's task was soon finished, and by November, they were reassigned to Fort Shaw. From there, Faye Roe was called back East by the illness of his father, Admiral Francis Asbury Roe. Two months later, he returned to Fort Shaw, and they remained there for most of 1882.

As it had happened on a number of occasions, Frances and 2nd Lt. Roe were ousted from their quarters when a senior officer moved onto their post. It happened on nearly every post they had been—and it happened at Fort Shaw in November, 1882. This time, it seemed worse. Their cellar was full of vegetables for the winter; the house was cleaned and painted; the floors were painted and hand-oiled. Lt. and Mrs. Roe had to move into two rooms and a shed.

In March, 1883, after 12 years, Faye Roe was promoted to first lieutenant and transferred to Fort Ellis, Montana Territory. He was assigned to be post quartermaster and commissary.

That summer of 1883 was notable for two reasons. First, in July, a hailstorm with stones "the size of a hen's eggs," broke every window at Fort Ellis. Water forced gophers from their holes, and the hailstones killed hundreds of them. Quartermaster Roe telegraphed St. Paul headquarters, asking that they ship 900 panes of glass.

In August, the Roes traveled to Yellowstone Park in a party of a dozen. They spent several weeks there, camping on the Fire-Hole River, in a pine grove just above the Upper Falls of the Yellowstone, at Hell's Half Acre, in the pine forest back of Old Faithful and at the Mammoth Hot Springs. They returned from the park through Rocky Canyon.

Frances and Faye spent the winter in the East, but she was glad to return to Montana. She wrote, "I love army life here in the West and I love all the things that it brings to me—the grand mountains, the plains, and the fine hunting." She had enjoyed her trip East and said it refreshed her, but she added, "Citizens and army people have so little in common, and this one feels after being with them a while, no matter how near and dear the relationship may be. Why, one half of them do not know the uniform, and could not distinguish an officer of the Army from a policeman!"

First Lt. Roe was now the regimental adjutant, and during the summer of 1884, he reorganized the band. He received guidelines do so from the director of the Marine band, John Philip Sousa. Sousa, according to Mrs. Roe, wrote "The March Past of the Rifle Regiment" for her husband. The song, according to her, was "dedicated to the officers and enlisted men."

Four years later, in May of 1888, John Rutter Brooke (she disguises his name as Bourke) was promoted to brigadier general and given command of the Department of the Platte with headquarters in Omaha, Nebraska. Brooke appointed Faye Roe to be his aide-de-camp. She wrote, "These appointments are complimentary, and considered most desirable." On the other hand, she admitted, "It will be a wretched life for me—cooped up in a noisy city!" Later, she wrote, "I love the West and life at a Western post and the virtues of city life do not seem attractive to me." She added later on, "The one thing that distresses me most of all is, that I have to part from my horse!"

Still later, "We know that when we leave Fort Shaw we will go from the old army life of the West .... We have seen the passing of the buffalo and other game, and the Indian seems to be passing also."

The Paxton Hotel in Omaha became home for a while, and the heat the summer of 1888 was nearly unbearable. The serene beauty and quiet of the Montana mountains was replaced by the buzzing and clanging of electric streetcars. There was some relief when the Roes traveled west again aboard a train to the Uintah Mountains in present Utah. They visited various sites and ended up swimming in the Great Salt Lake, or rather, as Frances Roe pointed out, you could only float in the salty lake—with large straw hats on.

One of the last things that Frances Roe included in her manuscript was that she and Faye planned on spending the winter of 1888-89 in Washington, D.C.

Frances Roe's manuscript was complete and off to the publisher. It went on sale during 1909.

But Frances Roe left out perhaps the greatest part of this story of love. Her husband served his last 10 years in the service in various staff positions. He was named lieutenant colonel of staff and judge advocate and was transferred to the First Army Corps at Mobile, Alabama in 1898. Faye requested retirement just weeks later, in December 1898, and went directly to the Hot Springs,

Arkansas Army and Navy Hospital, suffering from a complete mental and physical collapse.

Faye and Frances Roe had no children, so together they moved to Port Orange, near present Daytona Beach, Florida, and there they lived out their last days. Frances did what she could to nurse Faye back to health, but nothing seemed to help. At the same time, her health began to slip.

Still bothered by gastritis and severe headaches, Faye, aged 66, chose a quiet Thursday, September 28, 1916, to shoot and kill himself. He was buried in Arlington National Cemetery.

For Frances, it must have been a hard time. She wrote once, "The fact of my having been at a military post when it was attacked by Indians—that a man was murdered directly under my window, when I heard every shot, every moan—and my having had two unpleasant experiences with horse thieves, has not been conducive to normal nerves after dark."

And now she had to face the tragedy of her life, the death of her beloved Faye. Still, in a style befitting her life, she only wrote, "We had been good comrades forty-five years, and now it seems as though I was breaking faith with him to live on."

Mrs. Frances Roe died on May 6, 1920, and is buried beside her beloved husband at Arlington.

7

Kitty LeRoy: "The Cause of The Tragedy—Jealously"

Kitty LeRoy stepped across the small room to the door. Kitty's room was upstairs over the Lone Star Saloon. She slipped the latch and tugged the door open, her brown, curly hair tousled and shining, her bright, grey eyes smiling. When she saw who stood in the hall, the smile slid away, replaced almost by a grimace. It was Sam, Sam Curley! He was back.

Kitty blurted an uncomfortable greeting and forced another smile onto her face. This was trouble; she knew it the moment she saw him. He slid past her into the drafty room. Kitty hesitated, but then shoved the door shut.

It was December 1877, and Deadwood City, Dakota Territory, was a town that had everything. In the summer, men panned for gold in the "suburbs" or visited a public bath house. Variety theaters like the Bella Union or the Gem where scattered along Main Street. There were gambling halls, cribs, drinking dives and a Grand Central Hotel. In establishments like the Bucket of Blood, or Montana, or Nuttall's, or Mann's No. 10, or the Green Front Sporting House, there was everything a man needed to stay alive—or get killed.

Shut in by wooded hills, one visitor described the town as being "about three miles long and fifty feet wide." Included in the few thousand inhabitants were gold miners, adventurers, gamblers, harlots and dancing girls.

Just a year earlier, a correspondent named James Finerty observed, "Women, as in Cheyenne, acted as dealers at many of the tables and more resembled incarnate fiends than did their vulture-like male associates. I observed that decided brunettes were more engaged in evil works than their negative fellow-women."

Of another woman in Deadwood, Finerty observed: "Her eye glittered like that of a rattlesnake and she raked in the gold dust or chips with hands whose long white fingers, sharp at the ends, reminded one of a harpy's talons."

Laid out on April 26, 1876, Deadwood was organized about five and one-half months later. One described it as a town where "Sunday is no better than any other day, and every other day is as bad as it can be, but night is still worse." Another claimed that Deadwood was "a place where no man dies except with his boots on."

And Kitty LeRoy, in the fall of 1877, was a big part of all that was wild and crazy about the frontier town. Facts about Kitty are as tough to come by as an honest hand of poker in 1870s Deadwood. One correspondent wrote: "Barring the wild, Gypsy-like attire, Kitty LeRoy was what a real man would call a starry beauty. Her brow was low, and her brown hair thick and curling; she had five husbands, seven revolvers, a dozen bowie-knives, and always went armed to the teeth, which later were like pearls set in coral. She was a terrific gambler, and wore in her ears immense diamonds, which shone almost like her glorious eyes. The magnetism about her marvelous beauty was such as to drive her lovers crazy; more men had been killed about her than all the other women in the hills combined, and it was only a question whether her lovers or herself had killed the most.

"She could throw a bowie-knife straighter than any pistol bullet, except her own, and married her first husband because he was the only man of all her lovers who had the nerve to let her shoot an apple off his head while she rode by at full speed. On one occasion she disguised herself in male attire to fight a man who refused to combat with a woman. He fell, and she then cried, and married him in time to be his widow. Kitty was sometimes rich and sometimes poor, but always lavish as a prince when she had money. She dealt 'vantoon' and 'faro,' and played all games and cards with dexterity that amounted to genius."

Truth or fiction? Some claim she was married to a Captain E.H. Lewis of Bay City, Michigan and had taken their son and left him in 1872 when she was perhaps 23 years of age. Others claim she entered "upon her wild career at the age of ten."

One witness claimed that she was small, with "a large Roman nose; cold, grey eyes; a low cunning forehead." And she had several husbands "and then when their money was gone, discarded them in rapid succession." According to another story, she took a German for $8,000, then beat him over the head and kicked him out.

Kitty showed up in Dallas, Texas, at Johnnie Thompson's Variety Theatre on Main Street during the winter of 1875-76. She was a "jig dancer" there and acquired a reputation "by her artistic dancing and gay rollicking and dashing manners." She created a furor in Dallas, not by her beauty, "but by the naivete of her manner, the personal magnetism that was peculiarly her own, and her charming winning ways."

Sometime early in 1876, Kitty ran off with a "well known saloon man." Together, they traveled to California, then sometime later, perhaps during 1877, arrived in Deadwood. Apparently she left her son in California.

In Deadwood, Kitty danced at the Gem Theater and "presided" at the Mint Gambling Saloon, where "she was an expert in relieving miners of their gold."

Somehow, Kitty got tangled up with Samuel R. Curley, a noted faro dealer who was well known throughout the West. One wrote, "Curley was about 35 years of age, and had the reputation of a peaceful individual."

Kitty had taken up with Curley after ditching the "well known saloon man" and some say she even married Curley in Deadwood on the stage of the Gem Theatre. For some reason Curley departed for Denver and Kitty once again took up with the saloon man. When Curley found out, he grabbed a stagecoach for the trip back to Deadwood.

Sam Curley stepped down from the Cheyenne stage on December 5, 1877, probably about 6 p.m. He got off in South Deadwood and told the driver not to mention that he was in town. He walked directly to the Lone Star Saloon where he climbed the narrow, dark stairs to Kitty's room. There, Sam Curley remained.

Sam had murder in mind. He sent for the "saloon man" who refused to come. He boasted to a black man at the hotel that he planned on killing his wife and himself.

The landlady heard them having "slight quarrels" on the evening of December 6, "at 7 o'clock," she recalled. Then Kitty borrowed money from the landlady and gave it to Curley. Kitty told the landlady that Sam planned on taking the stage for Cheyenne the next morning.

It was not long until, according to the landlady, "The two were engaged in a low conversation up stairs when Kitty uttered a scream which was followed by two pistol shots."

The first ones to scramble up the narrow, dark stairs and through the hall into the room probably knew what they would find. Sam Curley was over there. He lay face down, his feet not a yard from Kitty's. She was on her back. Curley lay in "a sickening pool of blood, his brain oozing out and pieces of his skull protruding from a ghastly wound. His right arm was doubled up behind him, the hand grasping a Smith & Wesson, by which the fatal deed was committed." It was a .44 calibre, American model, Smith & Wesson.

A Dr. Conley arrived and found that the bullet hole in the waist of Kitty's dress "disclosed the fatal wound in the center of her chest." The bullet that killed Kitty LeRoy passed through her, shattered a window and thudded into a building across the street.

One newsman wrote of Kitty LeRoy "lying dead by the inanimate body of her husband, with whom she would not live but with whom she was obliged to pass quietly to the grave."

Another wrote, "The cause of the tragedy may be summed up in a few words: aye, in one—'jealously.' "

The bodies were prepared and laid out for friends to visit by the next morning. Undertaker Charles Storm was in charge of arrangements. The corpses were on display in the front room over the Lone Star Saloon where they had died.

On the morning of Saturday, December 8, Deadwood residents and passers-by crowded into the Lone Star Saloon for the funeral. The Congregational minister, the Reverend Mr. Norcross, quieted the group and led them in prayer. He then opened his Bible to a marked page, read a passage of scripture and made a few remarks. The funeral was done.

If there were tears for Kitty and Sam no one mentioned it. Kitty LeRoy and Sam Curley were buried side by side.

8

Death Visits Miss Hamilton's House for "Working Girls"

The Old West was a harsh, unforgiving stage on which many players risked their lives in the 19th Century. These players, ordinary people looking for a better life, struggled to survive, living on the edge, coaxing life from frontier jobs in frontier towns and too often finding only that they had lost the gamble to the wiliest frontiersman of them all, Mr. Death.

Frontier life was a harsh, unforgiving environment wrought with hardships, especially for single women. Most women in the West understood this. The conventional way to get a man, of course, was to marry. And the Old West was a fine place to get married. One girl wrote a friend in the East, "Tell the girls that this is the greatest place for marrying they ever saw." Continuing, she emphasized, "You all think this is a joke, but I tell you 'tis the truth."

But in some cases, marriage did not fit the lifestyle. For those plying the trade of "the world's oldest profession," marriage was hardly the answer. Often, these women stayed in the trade only long enough to find a husband. Others, however, often had a steady man to take care of them when they were not working. Sometimes the arrangement was satisfactory. At other times, it became a fatal union.

An incident in Cheyenne, Wyoming Territory, just after midnight, the morning of October 29, 1879, was all too typical.

It was Indian summer, temperature in the 40s, too warm that night for Cheyenne in October. The moon shone brightly, lighting the streets of the little territorial capital created when the Union Pacific Railroad came to town a dozen years earlier in November 1867. And despite the stories visitors told about the wild, frontier town, it was taking on the look of a metropolis. There was an ornate opera house at the corner of Capitol Avenue and 17th Street. A beautiful Catholic Church stood at the corner of 19th and Ferguson. Two- and three-story buildings lined 16th from Capitol Avenue to Eddy Street. And preparations were underway for the visit of ex-President Ulysses S. Grant. He was due in town day after tomorrow.

Still, it had only been a few years since the Boston (Massachusetts) *Globe* had declared: "But one man has died at Cheyenne with his boots off since the town first sprouted, and he had them in his teeth and was crawling out a bedroom window, when an avenging pistol ball let daylight shine through him."

And now up in the vicinity of Ferguson and 18th Street, not far from the Presbyterian Church, and just after midnight, someone screamed. It came from Ida Hamilton's "house." Miss Hamilton's was not the only "house" around there. The yellow-haired women with store-bought complexions in their variegated clothes with bangle bracelets lived there. They were the "painted cats" Cheyenne visitors remembered in the 1870s. And they all looked alike, one observer claimed, what with their "chalk-white faces, scarlet-painted lips and cheeks, sometimes with a red feather or red bow on their hats, and leading a little dog on a leash."

For working girls, ladies of the night, like those at Ida Hamilton's, Tuesday night and Wednesday morning, October 29, 1879 was a "business" night. Then just before one a.m., there came the scream.

It came from a room upstairs at Ida's house. Downstairs a bearded Charles Boulter, a friend of Ida Hamilton's, sat in his room reading. He heard. Lee Marcl Rosseau, James Astarito and the man that kept the fruitstand on the corner were all downstairs. They too heard the woman's cry. Upstairs several of Miss Hamilton's girls, May West, Ida Moore and Florence Vaughn were startled by the horrible shriek.

The cry was filled with terror. It tore out of the house, across the yard, through the picket fence and into the street and neighborhood.

A man's voice roared through the narrow hallways and thin walls of the two-story house. He yelled, "I'll murder you!"

Then the woman, Ida Snow, screamed, sobbing, "Don't kill me! Don't kill me! For God's sake, help!"

By now Charles Boulter was at the stairs. He bounded up them two at a time, Miss Hamilton trailing along behind him, her skirts slowing her.

Upstairs, Boulter hesitated long enough to hear the direction of the struggle. Ida Moore stepped into the hall. She was all right. The struggle was in Ida Snow's room, he now realized.

In Ida Snow's room only minutes earlier, Edmund K. Malone (Some sources call him Edward H. Malone.) had begun quarreling with Snow.

Malone was an old friend. Miss Snow had lived with him for eight years. But when he was drinking, he was "very wicked, revengeful," she said later.

This fight started when Malone asked Ida if she'd voted in the special election on Tuesday. (The election was to fill a vacancy created when the county attorney died.) She had not voted and said so. For some reason, his rage grew and he struck her on the head several times. Malone shouted threats. He screamed "that he would cut me in two if he only had a knife," Snow remembered later. Then he demanded, "I'll give you just three minutes to get in that bed."

She said she wouldn't and Malone growled, "I wish I had a pistol; I'd kill you!" Instead, Malone pulled a "pen knife" from his pocket, opened it and told her he would cut her "from mouth down to stomach." Then he grabbed her by the neck and began choking her.

Boulter, finally at the door outside, pounded frantically, insisting he be let in. Malone had locked the door. Ida Hamilton screamed for Snow to open the door. Then, convinced Snow couldn't get to the door, Boulter kicked it in.

Across the small room, Malone held Ida Snow by the throat, his face twisted with rage. Blood trickled from her mouth, as Boulter wrenched Malone away from her. Malone was not a big man, but Boulter had trouble breaking his grip on Miss Snow's throat.

Malone, stunned at the intrusion, reeled, glaring wildly at his attacker. He reached to push his glasses back on his nose, but Boulter grabbed him. Malone got a handful of Boulter's beard and they struggled for several seconds before Boulter got the upper hand and shoved and threw Malone out of the bedroom door into the narrow hallway.

Up the hall, May West stuck her head out of the her bedroom, glaring at the furious Malone. Ida Moore, half in her room and half out, watched as Malone screamed at Boulter, "You goddamned son of a bitch; you'll die!"

Boulter shoved Malone toward the backstairs and forced him down them. At the bottom of the stairs, just before he stepped through the door onto the porch, Malone shouted, his voice wild and trembling, "You son of a bitch, I'll kill everyone in the house!"

Malone said he would be back in ten minutes. With his gun. He slammed the door, punctuating his threat, then stumbled into the street and headed downtown.

James Astarito heard all this and when someone said, "I wish somebody would notify the police," Astarito decided he would go after a policeman. He wanted out of this place anyhow. This is not what he came here for.

Boulter and Miss Hamilton saw to it that the door was locked. There was nothing left to do. Maybe Malone would go home and sleep it off. And then again, maybe he would not. Boulter returned to his room and commenced reading.

The minutes ticked off. No sounds except the clock in the next room. Nothing else inside or out. Ida Hamilton stood quietly near the front door, taking her eyes off the door and porch only long enough to glance uncertainly at the others. Florence Vaughn stood silently in the front parlor. Outside there was an eerie quiet. The moonlight splashed into the street. No one moved about.

Ida Snow, still trembling from her brush with death, began sobbing softly now, a trickle of blood still visible on the corner of her mouth. She had come downstairs with the others. Violence often visited this occupation they were in, but none grew accustomed to it.

Suddenly Malone was back! No one saw him come onto the porch; he just appeared. Violently, he shook the door and knob! In the dim glow, Ida Snow saw a pistol in his hand.

Then Malone was screaming and cursing, as if he could sense that they all stood frightened just inside the darkened house. Malone demanded that they come out so that he could kill them. He dared Boulter to come out, said he would shoot him on sight. Said if Boulter did not come out, he would shoot through the windows. Ida Hamilton remembered, "Boulter told him to put the pistol down, but he would not do it."

Florence Vaughn, alone in the Hamilton's front parlor when Malone began yelling and rattling the front door, fled upstairs where she could watch from the safety of her window. She looked onto the street and saw Malone there now.

He stood, feet spread, planted in the street, his pistol in his hand, the moonlight flashing off his pistol, then his glasses as he called wildly, "Boulter, bring out your shotgun." (Ida Hamilton said later that Boulter "always keeps a gun in my room.")

Without a sound, Boulter was suddenly gone. Ida Hamilton didn't see him go out. Lee Marcl Rosseau didn't hear him go out. But in the house next door, a place called "Jennie's," one of Jennie Mortimer's girls, Bessie Laurence, watched Boulter. She was sitting at her downstairs window when she heard Malone in the street. She heard him using "very profane language." Then, Bessie said, "After

Malone had talked for a time Boulter came out the side door with his gun." Quietly she watched Boulter through the open window. He stayed in the shadows about ten feet from the window where Bessie watched. Boulter was "about half way back to the south end of the house," Bessie said later.

From her window, Florence Vaughn still had a good view of Malone. He made a good target. He wore a light coat and dark pants. He was in the street, the moonlight still flashing off the pistol and his glasses, his head held high.

Ida Hamilton had moved to the dining room. She watched Malone in the street, in the moonlight. She saw the pistol in his hand and claimed later, "He pointed the pistol straight at Boulter."

Florence Vaughn tried to pick out Boulter. Her eyes swept the street and yard. "The blinds," she remembered later, "were tied up so that I could see between them. I saw no one but Malone. He was standing facing the northwest corner of Jennie's yard and had the pistol in his right hand," she recalled. "Malone was not quite in the middle of the street. He had his arm raised."

Ida Moore, watching Malone in the street too, noticed he was facing east. "I could tell by the flash of his eyeglasses."

Boulter, close to Jennie's house and in the shadows now, eyed Malone, visible past the fence and sidewalk in the moonlit street. He shouldered the big shotgun and jerked off a shot.

Florence Vaughn saw the flash from the yard. Like lightning, the blast sprayed light at the houses and yards. The fence lit up for an instant as the shotgun barked death into the night. "When the shot was fired," she recalled, "after the flash, Malone turned around— one leg flew up and he dropped."

Ida Moore saw Malone drop too, but she said, "I went away from the window to say something to some one and when I came back he was gone."

Charles Korengel, a neighbor across the street, peered out his window and saw what happened next: "After Malone was shot he fell in the middle of the street and afterwards jumped up and ran."

Actually, he ran to the corner of 18th and Ferguson before he fell near the Presbyterian Church where Reverend J.Y. Cowhick would, later that day, hold a prayer meeting. The topic: "Faith rooted in darkness."

Lee Marcl Rosseau was still inside Ida Hamilton's house when the shot was fired. Just seconds later he saw Boulter come into the house. "When he came in he went into another room," Rosseau recalled.

Ida Hamilton said to Boulter, "I didn't know you had your gun." He replied that "he had not intended of hitting him but thought he would scare him—that anyone who would beat a woman would be scared by a gun." Boulter admitted later that he "fired low to strike him in the legs." His gun was loaded with slugs, he told the police.

In the meantime, James Astarito, who'd gone looking for a policeman, found one. Policeman F.C. Thomason was standing in front of the Dyer's Hotel when Astarito told him, "There was a row in Ida Hamilton's." So Thomason, City Marshal Andrew Ryan and another policeman named E.H. Ingalls started up there.

They walked to the corner of Eddy and 17th and then across to Ferguson where they turned left up that street toward the trouble.

About halfway between 17th and 18th streets, Thomason heard the shotgun. He saw Malone walking west. Thomason testified later, "When he got about four or five feet from the corner of 18th and Ferguson street he fell."

Marshal Ryan said Malone must have walked fifty feet before he fell that second time.

A Stock Association detective, B.W. Morrison was coming on the scene too. He heard the commotion and claimed, "When I first saw Malone he was near the Presbyterian Church on the west side of the Church about ten feet up from where the 18th sidewalk crosses Ferguson."

Thomason said, "I ran to him and asked him what was the matter—he made no reply. I found that he had a pistol jutting under him. The pistol was cocked. I heard the pistol fall."

When Morrison got to him, Malone was lying on his back. Morrison recalled, "He did not speak at that time. He was bleeding at the mouth."

Thomason, after he took away the pistol, noted, "I ran across the street to find the man that done the shooting."

Korengel came out of his house and pointed Thomason in the direction of the flash. Thomason headed for Ida Hamilton's yard. Boulter was outside again and said, "I am the man that did the shooting." He gave himself up to Marshal Ryan and Thomason.

Returning to Malone in the street, Thomason and the others picked Malone up and carried him down to Hurlbut's Drug Store. They sent for the doctor.

"Before the doctor got there," Thomason recalled, "we partly examined him (Malone) and found where one shot had come through the groin. When the doctor came we turned him over on his side and we found six wounds, I think."

The Stock Association detective, B.W. Morrison was there too. "I saw all the wounds there on his body—there were two shot wounds near the coupling of the back bone—one wound was about the centre of the back—there were two in his side—the others were in his side pretty low down."

When Dr. E.B. Graham arrived from his home at 402 16th Street, Malone was "lying on his back in an unconscious condition." Graham said, "There was no pulse at the wrist and he was unable to speak."

The doctor tried to probe the wounds, but it caused Malone pain, so he quit and had Malone moved to a little house "north of Recreation Hall" where Malone had rooms.

J.H. Larkin, a friend of Malone's and a local barkeep, had come to the drug store and questioned Malone about the shooting. Morrison heard and testified later, "Malone would not tell who shot him but said they came up and shot him in the back."

Larkin, who used the alias, J.H. Nicholson, added though, "He may have said that he was shot in the back merely from braggadocio as he generally wanted it understood that he was a bad man."

Dr. Graham noted that Malone had been drinking. Graham said later, "He seemed to suffer considerably—he complained of great pain in his bowels and he vomited." Later, Graham recalled, "I helped him up and considerable blood passed his bowels. He seemed very much depressed. He wanted to know what I thought of his chances. I told him that if he had any requests to make or word to send he had better attend to them. He had no requests."

A knock on the door about three a.m. admitted Ida Snow, the prostitute Malone had tried to kill. She felt badly about it all; after all she'd been with Malone for eight years. They'd only been in Cheyenne since the first of the month, having arrived from Bodie, California. Malone often posed as a mining stock broker. Snow worked wherever she could. Most figured Malone lived off Snow, his "wife." She looked at him for a few minutes and decided there was little else she could do. She shook her head. He was a wicked, treacherous man, she told herself, especially when he was drinking. She left.

About four a.m., Dr. Graham went home. Larkin stayed with Malone. He said later, "Malone knew that he was going to die and repeatedly expressed himself to that effect. I was lying along side of him when he died."

The funeral of 30-year-old Edward H. Malone took place the afternoon of October 30, but sleet and snow followed a blast of raw, cold wind and dropping temperatures delayed the burial until the next day. Ida Snow paid the burial expenses, including the five dollar burial fee.

Item: Cheyenne *Daily Leader*, October 31, 1879: "Charles Boulter, charged with killing E.H. Malone, was taken before Justice Bean yesterday afternoon, when he waived the preliminary examination, and on the consent of Acting County Attorney Potter, his bail was fixed at $5,000. The bond was given and the prisoner was released."

Less than a year later, on August 14, 1880, Ida Snow was buried beside Malone. Cause of death: "Apoplexy." She was 28 years old.

Mr. Death had won again.

9

In the Shadow:
The Story of Josephine Marcus Earp

The story of Western woman is often told only in the shadow of her man's adventures. While a bone-weary miner scraped and picked a great hole in the earth, struggling to find just one more nugget of gold, or just one more rock laden with silver ore, somewhere a woman, his woman waited.

And while an exhausted young soldier, in the midst of an Indian attack, fought bravely for his life, his blue, wool uniform nearly strangling him with sweat and heat, somewhere a woman, his woman waited.

Or when a lean, straight gunfighter stepped into a dusty street, his cold-steel eyes squinting at the bright, hot sun, his gun hand ready to deliver death, somewhere a woman, his woman, waited.

Some of these women were wives; some were not. All were willing to keep up with—or keep track of—their men. The West of the 1800s was full of such women, women willing to keep pace with their men, each apparently satisfied to live in the shadow of her man's adventures.

Living in the shadow was something Josephine Marcus Earp did well. From the early 1880s for nearly a half-century, this dark,

The last wife of Wyatt Earp,
Josephine Marcus Earp.
(Author's Collection)

beautiful woman from Brooklyn, by way of San Francisco, lived in the shadow of one of the wild and woolly West's greatest legends.

And then in January, 1929, it was all over.

While living in a rented, three-room cottage in a Los Angeles tourist court at 4004 West 17th Street, Josephine Earp was suddenly alone. At 8:05 on the morning of January 13, 1929, just over two months short of his 81st birthday, Wyatt Berry Stapp Earp died. "My darling," she wrote, "had breathed his last, dying peacefully, without a struggle, like a baby going to sleep."

Josephine, now in her late 60s, was devastated. She did not attend the funeral. "I was adrift—a rudderless ship," she recalled. "Loneliness follows you wherever you go after you've lost the love of your life."

But she had memories and after a while, they became the stuff that made life worth living again. And soon, she had a desire to tell her story and Wyatt's.

Stuart Lake's *Wyatt Earp, Frontier Marshal* did not set well with her and when Hollywood attempted to make a movie of the same name, she let it be known that she opposed it. A 1939 movie based on the book kept the name "Frontier Marshal," but the main character, Randolph Scott, was not called Wyatt Earp.

In collaboration with Earp kinsmen, related by marriage, Josephine wrote about 400 pages of her story between 1936 and

1944. Nearly a quarter-century after her death, this material became the property of author Glenn G. Boyer. From that and numerous other sources, Boyer edited *I Married Wyatt Earp: The Recollection of Josephine Sarah Marcus Earp*.

Josephine Marcus was the third wife of famed frontiersman, businessman, miner, lawman, gunfighter, gambler and saloon keeper Wyatt Berry Stapp Earp.

Wyatt Earp was 21 when he married his first wife, Urilla Sutherland, at Lamar, Missouri. She died in childbirth during 1870. The child also died.

Sometime between 1870 and late 1879, Earp took up with Celia Ann (Mattie) Blaylock. Were they married? There is no official record of marriage, but theirs may have been a common law marriage. Those who knew Mattie and Wyatt in 1880, considered them man and wife.

It was while Wyatt Earp lived in Tombstone, Arizona, that he left Mattie for wife number three, Josephine Marcus. (No evidence exists of a divorce having taken place between Wyatt and Mattie.)

Josephine Sarah Marcus lived in San Francisco. She moved there from Brooklyn, New York, with her prosperous, German-Jewish parents, Hyman and Sophia Marcus, in the late 1860s. Josephine was only seven when her family sailed from New York to Panama, across the isthmus and by ship to San Francisco.

When she was 18 years of age, Josephine grew restless. She wrote of the time, "My blood demanded excitement, variety and change."

Gilbert and Sullivan's musical, *H.M.S. Pinafore*, was playing in San Francisco. Josephine attended the theater many times and was fascinated by the musical. She wanted to be a part of the show. When Pauline Markham took the troupe of *H.M.S. Pinafore* on the road, young Josephine left home to accompany the show.

Traveling in two coaches, the troupe of 26 actors and actresses made its way south through California and finally into central

Arizona. There, in Arizona, Josephine met the deputy sheriff of Yavapai County, 34-year-old John Behan.

Their meeting and subsequent courtship turned into a whirlwind romance and netted her a diamond ring and a promise of marriage. Josephine then returned to San Francisco to ask for her parents' consent to marry Behan. This accomplished, she prepared to travel to Tombstone where Behan had moved in anticipation of being appointed sheriff of Cochise County.

Josephine rode a train that summer of 1880, to within 20 or 25 miles of Tombstone, to the little town of Benson, Arizona. From there, Josephine caught a stagecoach to Tombstone. The trip by stage to Tombstone was along a dusty, crowded road. Ore and freight wagons obstructed the road and the stage driver whipped his team past the slower wagons, throwing clouds of powdery, hot dust into the air. Just outside Tombstone, John Behan met the stage.

Tombstone lay spread over a plateau between the Dragoon and Whetstone Mountains in southeast Arizona's San Pedro Valley. The town was suffering a silver-mining boom begun in 1877 by a miner born in Pittsburgh, Pennsylvania, Edward L. Schieffelin.

At the time of Josephine's arrival, Tombstone was a collection of frame structures and adobe buildings. She also noticed "a good number of tents here and there." All sorts of wagons and buggies cluttered the streets, and there were horses, burros, dogs and chickens everywhere. Later, she wrote, "My mother would have fainted if she knew what sort of place Tombstone really was."

She and Behan's life together began there that summer and after a few months, with Behan's interest in her in doubt, she inquired as to his intentions.

Behan, his slim face twisted, said as calmly as possible, "We can't afford to get married yet."

If it was money that was slowing the process, Josephine decided, then she would send to San Francisco and ask her father for money.

A short time later, when Josephine received the money, she pawned her diamond ring and gave all the money to Behan. Behan, according to her, used the money to build a small frame house on the northeast corner of Seventh and Stafford in Tombstone.

Still, no marriage.

Sometime during the late summer or fall of 1880, Josephine Marcus met Wyatt Earp. Earp, like Behan, hoped to be appointed Cochise County Sheriff. In January 1881, Earp lost out as Behan received the sheriff's appointment.

Josephine was impressed with Earp. "Wyatt was a handsome man," she wrote. "He was tall with a trim, erect figure, and he was unusually muscular and powerful for his build. He was also quick and graceful as a cat. His dress was always neat but inconspicuous. His habits of grooming and personal cleanliness were all any woman could hope for in her ideal."

One night then, Behan came home drunk and made improper passes at Josephine. She decided then that she would take back her house from Behan. With that decision, she also opened the way for Wyatt Earp to come courting.

Josephine knew Wyatt was "married" to Mattie Blaylock at the time, but she wrote later, "It was no secret that his marriage was on the rocks." And that was enough reason for her to set her hat for Wyatt.

As far as John Behan was concerned, Josephine said, "He did me just one favor. Through him I met Wyatt Earp."

Wyatt Earp, her last love, was everything she hoped for. For almost 50 years from that time, Josephine was Wyatt's woman and companion. And to Josephine, he "was a real warm-hearted, flesh-and-blood man."

In their Tombstone days, Wyatt Earp was a businessman. He owned and operated various gambling interests in Tombstone. In addition, he and his brothers scoured the surrounding area for mining interests, timber to file on, and suitable water and mineral claims. Josephine claimed, "Wyatt was above all a level-headed businessman with an eye on the future."

"One of the first things Wyatt told me when our courtship started," Josephine remembered, "was that the Earps had decided to stay in Tombstone with part of their long-range plan being to capture the lucrative steady income from the sheriff's office."

And this might have come to pass, except for the events of Wednesday, October 26, 1881. On that day in Tombstone, the day of the infamous, so-called "Gunfight at the O.K. Corral," the direction of the lives of the Earp brothers and most others involved in the gunfight was changed.

Prior to this date, there had been a long-running feud between the Earp faction and the Clanton-McLaury group. Still controversial, some believe the Clanton-McLaury side was upset because the Earps were cutting themselves in on the Clanton's and McLaury's stage holdups and cattle rustling. Others argue that the Earps were actually trying to break up the illegal activities of the Clantons and McLaurys.

Whatever the reasons, Josephine knew there was going to be a fight. A woman named Marietta Spence had warned her that Ike Clanton and Frank McLaury planned to kill the Earps in a "fair fight." She relayed this to Wyatt. Following this, as she wrote later, "There was nothing I could do but wait and pray."

Not long after noon on October 26, Wyatt and Morgan Earp and their brother, Chief of Police Virgil Earp, met in front of Hafford's Saloon on the northeast corner of Fourth and Allen. Soon joining them was John H. "Doc" Holliday. (Josephine: Doc Holliday was "a well-educated, consumptive, frontier bum.") A short time later, the Earps and Holliday walked toward Fremont Street.

At the corner of Fourth and Fremont, the men turned left and walked along Fremont toward Third. Near the corner of Third, between Camillus Fly's Photograph Gallery and part-time rooming house and William Harwood's frame house, the Earps and Holliday confronted Ike and Billy Clanton, Tom and Frank McLaury and Billy Claiborne. City Ordinance Number Nine prohibited the wearing of guns in Tombstone except when leaving city limits. There was no mention of the ordinance.

There, in a space less than 20 feet wide, Virgil Earp stopped within six feet of the Clantons. Wyatt, Doc Holliday and Morgan Earp stood near the edge of the street facing the McLaurys. In just seconds, the killing space between the buildings was filled with hot lead and clouds of gunsmoke. Billy Clanton slammed up against Harwood's house. He died. Ike ran. Tom McLaury took a shotgun blast that started him into the street where he died. Frank McLaury was hit, down and dying. Billy Claiborne, like Ike, ran away before anyone could draw a bead on him.

When the smoke cleared, Virgil Earp was down, shot in the calf of his leg. A slug had drilled Morgan's shoulder. Doc Holliday was hit in the hip. Of the Earp and Holliday wounds, none were fatal.

Josephine, Wyatt's woman, was in her house at Seventh and Stafford during all this. She recalled, "I jumped up as I heard the firing start. A picture flashed through my mind of Wyatt falling before the gunfire of Johnny's (Behan) horrible poker-playing cronies."

In a panic, she remembered, "I could scarcely breathe. Without stopping for a bonnet I rushed outside and toward the sound of the firing before it died down."

In her excitement, Josephine guessed there must have been 100 shots fired. (*The Tombstone Nugget* reported 30 shots in 25 seconds.) When she reached Fremont Street, she looked three blocks up the street to where people had begun to cluster near the newspaper office, *The Tombstone Epitaph*. Gasping for air, she began running, her long skirt beating against her legs.

A wagon pulled alongside and the driver called out, "Hop in, lady—I'll run you up to the excitement."

The man whipped the team into a gallop and reined them to a halt as Josephine recklessly leaped to the ground. The wounded Virgil and Morgan were being helped onto another wagon. She glanced frantically around, wondering where Wyatt had gone.

Then she saw him. She wrote later, "I almost swooned when I saw Wyatt's tall figure very much alive, starting up Fremont with Doc and Fred Dodge on the opposite side of the street."

Wyatt saw her and stepped into the street, walking toward her. "My God," she remembered thinking, "I haven't got a bonnet on. What will they think?" She concluded, "I was simply a little hysterical."

The shooting, the affair of October 26, 1881, was not finished. An inquest cleared the Earp bunch of any wrongdoing, but threats erupted against Judge Wells Spicer, the Earps, Holliday, Editor John Clum of the pro-Earp *Tombstone Epitaph* and Wyatt's lawyer, Tom Fitch.

There were incidents, but none of significance until about one-half hour short of midnight on December 28, 1881. From a building soon to be the Huachuca Water Company at the southeast corner of Fifth and Allen, several shotgun blasts roared in the night, spinning Virgil Earp in the cold, dark street and dropping him to the ground. He staggered to his feet, his left arm and leg oozing blood, and attracted by the dim light from the Oriental Saloon, reeled into the saloon before collapsing. Patrons in the saloon carried Earp to the Cosmopolitan Hotel where he remained until March. He recovered from his injuries.

Wyatt, at the time, told Josephine that he figured he had three choices: "Break the back of the Rustler organization, leave the country, or be assassinated."

Then, on March 18, 1882, about 10:30 p.m., Wyatt's mind was made up for him. He and brother Morgan were in Campbell and Hatch's Billiard Parlor on Allen Street just east of the Alhambra Saloon. From outside, at the rear, a shot was fired through a glass door and into the right side of Morgan Earp's abdomen. The bullet passed through the spinal column, completely shattering it, before emerging on the left side. George A.B. Berry stood at the other end of the room by the stove. The same bullet that hit Earp struck Berry in the thigh, but only left him with a flesh wound.

A second shot, fired instantly after the first, was found in the wall near the ceiling over the head of Wyatt Earp. He had been sitting watching the game.

The lives of Wyatt and Josephine changed quickly. Morgan died, and Wyatt insisted on revenge. Josephine was under considerable pressure to return to San Francisco. Even though her parents did not know of her relationship to Wyatt, they read all about Tombstone in the newspapers and feared for their daughter in such a wild, lawless town.

She pleaded with Wyatt to go with her. All she could think of was: "Would Wyatt be next?" He would not go with her, but did leave Tombstone on March 21. He had business to finish. And besides, as she recalled later, "He was not a runner. He was the bravest man I ever knew."

Josephine stayed around for a few days, but then departed for San Francisco. "I left Tombstone," she wrote, "with a sense of relief, glad that Wyatt had got safely away, and relieved to be away from the dreadful place myself. It had come to mean nothing but suppressed terror to me."

A few weeks later, Wyatt showed up in San Francisco. Josephine, after the calm and sanity of San Francisco, was ready, she recalled, for "excitement, variety and change."

Josephine wrote, "One of the first things we realized we had in common was an insatiable desire to travel—to see new people and places." Off they went to Gunnison, Colorado, "by way of Salt Lake City and Denver." From Denver, she sometimes accompanied Wyatt on hunting and fishing trips. At other times, she attended parties and moved in Denver social circles to occupy her time while Wyatt was gone. She liked Denver; it was a nice town.

In 1883, they traveled to one of Wyatt's former towns, Dodge City. She did not think much of it and wrote, "It looked like all the other rundown prairie towns."

They returned to Colorado then on to Texas before the end of 1883. Wyatt made, according to her, "a good living through investments or gambling." And she loved this traveling life.

Early in 1884, Josephine and Wyatt headed for Shoshone County, Idaho, and the Coeur d' Alene District gold strike. Wyatt was involved in several enterprises in Idaho, including a saloon called the "White Elephant." Before long though, he and Josephine were off to Fort Worth, El Paso, Austin, San Antonio and Laredo, Texas.

Josephine claimed that Wyatt worked for Wells Fargo and gambled. And according to her, they were as "carefree as honeymooners." (Josephine claimed, by the way, that she and Wyatt were married while aboard millionaire Elias Jackson "Lucky" Baldwin's yacht in international waters.)

After Texas, Josephine and Wyatt returned to California. Wyatt's parents lived in Colton, California, and after a stop there, they traveled to San Diego and lived there for a while. In San Diego, Wyatt was involved in, among other things, real estate and horse racing.

Wyatt drove a rubber-tired sulky in trotting races and won a horse named "Jim Leach" in a poker game. Between 1885 and 1897, he owned and raced a half-dozen horses. He and Josephine took their horses to the World's Columbian Exposition in Chicago in 1893 and raced his horses in such cities as Cincinnati, St. Louis and Kansas City.

Involved in other sporting events, Wyatt was in San Francisco on December 2, 1896, to referee a heavyweight bout between Tom Sharkey and Bob Fitzsimmons. Fitzsimmons became the world heavyweight champion the next year.

Josephine and Wyatt were in southwest Arizona at Yuma when word came that there had been a gold strike in the Klondike. Before 1897 was out, they were in Alaska. The next year, before they could leave for the gold country, Wyatt suffered a dislocated hip. And Josephine became pregnant, but miscarried.

Josephine's Alaskan miscarriage was her second, the first coming while they lived in San Diego. This time, they decided to return to San Francisco for a rest. Josephine wrote, "Apparently God didn't make me right for having children, though we both loved them and longed for some of our own."

Soon, they returned to Alaska and rented a cabin in Rampart City on the Yukon River near Big Minook Creek. They were about 100 miles northwest of Fairbanks in a fairly good gold range. Their cabin was chinked with moss, and in the spring Wyatt planted a garden on the dirt roof. For this, they paid rent of $100 per month. Josephine wrote, "We considered ourselves lucky to get anything at any price."

There was a packing-box table and a small, iron cookstove. Their bed was of spruce poles with rope for springs. Over that was a mattress of fur robes. "I was happy as a queen," Josephine wrote, "because I was with Wyatt."

There were two other women who lived nearby and they and Josephine met over coffee from time to time and on occasion took night sleigh rides on the frozen Yukon River.

The Earps left Rampart City in July, 1899, and traveled to the port city of Saint Michael about 150 miles southeast and across Norton Sound from Nome. Saint Michael was a clean, law-abiding, harbor town with no mosquitoes, a fact that Josephine appreciated after fighting the pesky insects while they lived inland.

At Saint Michael, Wyatt operated a canteen for a 10 percent cut. Beer sold for $1 and cigars were 50 cents apiece. Hundreds were in Saint Michael, waiting to head for either Nome or the Klondike. Wyatt's canteen took in, according to Josephine's recollection, $2,000 a day.

Friends began urging Wyatt to come to Nome. He could triple his income, they promised. And so, it was off to Nome for the Earps. Nome, of course, had the look of a boom town. Josephine called it "a messy sprinkling of tents and half dozen very rough lumber shacks." The tents, she observed, were strung along the beach for "twenty miles." Running parallel to this string of tents was a muddy street behind and the beach in front. A sign on the street proclaimed:

THIS STREET IS IMPASSABLE—
NOT EVEN JACK-ASSABLE.

Wyatt went to work building Nome's first two-story structure, the Dexter Saloon. The second floor had 12 clubrooms; the saloon was downstairs. It was to be a splendid building. Just now, however, someone needed to go to the States and fetch back saloon furniture.

It was the excuse Josephine and Wyatt needed. They would go to Seattle. Besides, there was a typhoid outbreak in Alaska. And everyone said there was going to be a miserably cold winter.

Their boat ride to Seattle was no cruise. The ship was bug-infested, but they landed safely and wintered with friends in San Francisco and Denver. In July, 1900, while in Denver, word reached them that Wyatt's little brother, 35-year-old Baxter Warren Earp, had been shot to death in southeast Arizona at Willcox. Apparently, Baxter, while drinking, challenged a cowboy named John Boyett. Baxter, too drunk to remember that he was not wearing a gun, was killed.

Wyatt sent Josephine to San Francisco. He then traveled to Willcox where he met his brother, Virgil. They took care of their brother's affairs. Rumors over the years indicated that the brothers may have "taken care of" their brother's killer, while other sources claim that Boyett was acquitted of any crime.

After matters were settled in Willcox, Wyatt rejoined Josephine in San Francisco and they returned to Nome and the Dexter Saloon. Josephine wrote, "It was the most fashionable saloon in town and would have been a standout even in San Francisco." Wyatt liked to advertise it as: "The Only Second-Class Saloon in Alaska."

Business was good. One visitor, their old friend, "Lucky" Baldwin, recalled that Wyatt's place was the center of business. He wrote, "A few blocks away from Earp's saloon, in any direction, business simply petered out, and gave place to cabins and shacks occupied by residents of the camp, good, bad and indifferent."

Over the next months, Wyatt did well financially, but the "excitement, variety and changes" Josephine longed for were not there. "By the summer of 1901," Josephine complained, "our life had become routine. We were getting rich, but we were also getting bored."

That fall, Josephine and Wyatt boarded the S.S. *Roanoke*, headed for the United States. With the money Wyatt had made, they decided to look for ore in the West and, at the same time, search out a ranch site. What they did the most, however, was to travel around, usually ending up in Los Angeles when the deserts of Arizona, Nevada and California grew too hot.

Wyatt ran a saloon called "The Northern" in Tonopah, Nevada, for a time and, in 1903, tried homesteading. By 1915, he was mining in the Whipple Mountains in southeast San Bernardino County, California. Still prospecting into the late 1920s, the Earps filed nearly 100 claims and continued to load up their spring wagon with essentials and drive into the desert until July, 1928.

But the end of the trail was coming for the two. Wyatt was 80 years old now and they were living in a rented, three-room cottage in a Los Angeles tourist court at 4004 West 17th Street. At 8:05 on January 13, 1929, just over two months short of his 81st birthday, Wyatt Berry Stapp Earp died.

When Josephine recovered, she took Wyatt's ashes to San Francisco to be interred at the Hills of Eternity Cemetery in Colma. There, in December, 1944, after her death on December 19, Josephine joined Wyatt again, for all eternity.

10

Mary Clementine Collins:
Missionary to the Sioux

The Hunkpapa Sioux cabin settlement of Flying By was Sitting Bull's home on the Grand River in 1890. The old Sioux medicine man led his band of followers to Canada after the Custer Fight on the Little Big Horn in 1876 but returned to the United States in 1881. In 1883, after two years of imprisonment, he and his family returned to Standing Rock Reservation. Later on, they moved down on the Grand River in what is now South Dakota, built a double log cabin, and commenced raising cattle and chickens.

Approaching the camp in the fall of 1890 was a team and wagon. A Sioux man drove, holding the horses well in hand. A white woman dressed in black was seated alongside. Looking above the collection of crude log cabins and to the north they saw brown, grass-covered high hills. South along the river, naked cottonwoods stood shining in the morning sun. Clumps of willow trees clung to their last fall leaves. Beyond the half dozen mud-chinked log cabins, a cluttered village of poor canvas tipis circled a flat, bare area.

Assorted chickens pecked the hard ground, interrupted now and then by a litter of yipping puppies. The chickens fled just out of range of the pups, then resumed their nervous pecking. Scruffy

Sitting Bull
(U.S. Signal Corps)

adult dogs indifferently took that all in. Most claimed a place in the sun and ignored the team and wagon rolling into camp.

The man and woman looked around and saw a prayer tree—a tall pole decorated with multi-colored flags—rearing defiantly from the ground. Around the tree, the Sioux Ghost Dancers flaunted old-time war dress and paint and feathers. Even the women, each with a white feather tied in her hair, wore paint. Their heads back, they chanted, eyes fixed on the sun. Others stood around the dance circle, colorful shawls pulled over their heads against the morning chill.

The Ghost Dance medicine man Kicking Bear had carried the new religion to the desperate people at Sitting Bull's Grand River camp in October 1890. The Ghost Dance religion taught that the Messiah had come to earth again, this time as an Indian. He would resurrect all important things, the buffalo and antelope, relatives and friends. For many Sioux, these were exciting, hopeful days.

Mary Clementine Collins, the woman in the wagon, a Christian missionary, did not like what she saw. Continuing on, the wagon creaked toward the new out-station on the site of Sitting Bull's village. She came to lead mission services and worship Jesus Christ, not this Indian Christ that promised to raise up dead Indians, buffalo, antelope and deer.

Mary Collins' Christian services that morning drew only a few Sioux. Outside, the Ghost Dancers continued, their chanting growing louder. Collins recalled later the crude way the converts sang "Nearer My God to Thee" amid the chanting and screaming of the dancers at the prayer tree. "You could scarcely hear anything," she remembered.

After the services, she found the lodge of Sitting Bull, who was himself conducting ceremonies. Its entrance was guarded. She asked to be admitted. One of the young men ducked inside, then returned, refusing to admit her. "Not at this time," Sitting Bull had said. He performed a ritual. She understood but replied that she "wished most earnestly to talk with him."

She drew a deep sigh and waited patiently as a half hour came and went. When Sitting Bull finally asked for her, she ducked inside. He sat at the rear of the lodge behind a cool fire. With a motion of his hand, he directed her to circle to the right.

She had visited this council lodge before. Now, as then, she shook his left hand with her left hand. That earlier time, she tried to talk him out of the Ghost Dance, warning that "he might deceive a few Indians and a few white people, but that God could not be deceived." The old leader listened, full of wonder and interest. And she told him, solemnly, "My friend, I fear the time will come when you will remember with sorrow your work this day."

Since that earlier meeting, matters had worsened. A thousand dancers crowded Sitting Bull's village. The U.S. Army at Fort Yates flaunted weapons, intimidating the Sioux at the agency for ration allotments. That only excited Sitting Bull and his followers, fanning the flames of fear in their hearts. The Sioux stopped visiting the trading posts; they stopped working on the little farms; and they stopped sending their children to school.

Now Collins waited near Sitting Bull. He resumed his rites, ignoring her presence. She sat silent and thinking. After a while he asked her to speak.

"My brother," she began, "you are ruining your people; you are deceiving them and you know that you are. Go out and send them home," she pleaded, "before the soldiers come."

A smile softened the lines of his hard face and he shook his head. "My sister, I cannot do what you require. I have gone too far; they will laugh at me."

She seemed almost content with that response, but then she said, "Sitting Bull, you know you do not believe these things that you are telling your people; you know that the Indians have not risen from the death out in the White Mountains and that the buffalo and deer and your favorite hunting dogs are not alive again; you know that you are deceiving your people who have always trusted you."

Collins paused, then added, her voice firm, "The law orders you to go to Fort Yates and you must obey. You must go and talk with the officials there and tell them that you will have this dance cease. Otherwise the soldiers will come and kill all of your people. Your best warriors and men will be shot and the families will go unprovided for, and you, Sitting Bull, will be responsible for this terrible calamity. You must," she insisted, "send the people home."

As she spoke, the chanting outside grew louder and annoyed her even more. Sitting Bull's eyes left her face and rested on the fire until she finished. He remained a time in thought, then spoke, saying, "I cannot do it, my sister, but you do it. Tell them Sitting Bull said it."

Collins got to her feet, nodded to him, and walked around the fire and out of the big lodge. Outside a cold wind skipped dust through the dancers. She flew into the dance circle, scolding dancers as she pushed by them. They ignored her, continuing their chant: "The whole world is coming, A nation is coming, a nation is coming."

One of the dancers apparently fainted and fell to the ground. It was Sitting Bull's son, Louis. He looked unconscious, but Collins stooped, took him by the shoulders, and shook him, scolding him so that all heard. "Louis," she said sternly, "get up, you are not unconscious, you are not ill; get up and help me to send these people home."

The crowd hushed. The wind brought a chill over them. Louis grinned and his eyes opened wide. Slowly he climbed to his feet and looked around at the dancers. They began to scatter, leaving the dance circle.

Until the sun fell away that evening, Louis Sitting Bull and Mary Collins packed the Sioux Dancers into their wagons and started them toward their homes.

That visit to Sitting Bull's lodge was Mary Collins' last. Shortly

Sitting Bull's cabin at Flying By where he was killed.
(Author's collection)

before dawn on a frosty December 15, 1890, Sitting Bull was shot to death outside his cabin at Flying By. Collins always believed she was the last white person to see the great man alive.

The intrigue surrounding Sitting Bull's untimely death has been the subject of investigation, but what of this highly-educated, Christian woman living among the Sioux? Who was Mary Collins?

Mary Clementine Collins, born in Upper Alton, Illinois, on April 18, 1846, moved with her family to the newly chartered city of

A young Mary Clementine Collins.
(Courtesy of South Dakota State
Historical Society.)

Keokuk, Iowa, before her second birthday. A Sunday school teacher at Keokuk's First Congregational Church often told Mary's class, "I believe one of you will be a missionary, and so I think we will always pray to God to bless the one who is to be the Missionary." When old enough, Mary attended Ripon College in Wisconsin and earned a master's degree.

Back in Keokuk by 1872, Mary taught school. In 1875, she and a teacher friend, Emmarette Whipple, applied for a mission in Micronesia. Repeated bouts with pneumonia, however, made Mary a poor health risk. Finally, the society assigned Collins and Whipple to a mission among the Indians of Dakota Territory. She refused to go. Her mind was made up; she would not work among "those horrid Indians."

When Mary heard an Indian missionary, Nina Foster Riggs, speak, however, her mind was changed. Collins and Whipple rode a train to Chicago, joined missionaries Thomas and Nina Foster Riggs, and departed for Yankton, Dakota Territory. From there, they traveled by horse-drawn wagon through Santee, Nebraska, and on to Fort Sully. They arrived November 10, 1875, and went to work for the American Board, or the American Missionary Association.

Mary promised herself she would stay among the Indians for ten years only. From 1875 to 1885, she worked at the Oahe Mission in the Peoria Bottom of the Missouri River, an area one visitor called "a treeless waste under a scorching sun." The Indian language came almost instinctively to her, it seemed. Her Sioux assistant, Elizabeth Winyan, helped, too, and before long Mary conducted classes in the Sioux language, teaching day school and high school to all ages. Her knowledge of medicine helped her with the families. She claimed it was "more important to gain the friendship and love of some family than to teach a child in school."

For Mary Collins, the family visits were enjoyable but tiring. Of an 1876 visit, she wrote, "It is a lovely afternoon. The walk is a delightful one and we soon reach it (a village). The great number of dogs around each cabin would lead one to think the Dakota people held them sacred. In the first house we enter, we find a mother sitting on the bed, beading moccasins for her husband. Her little sick child is beside her, amusing himself with a clay horse which some of his playmates have made for him. On a blanket in one corner of the room sits another woman; she is a stranger. After leaving crackers for the sick child, promising medicine to another, and exchanging a few words, we go on...I frequently walked so much through the day, that at night I was too tired to sleep, and often I was so discouraged that I would lie awake to plan some more effective way of reaching the People."

When Mary's tenth year with the Indians rolled around, she had no intention of leaving them. So much had happened. Emmarette Whipple died after two years at the mission. Mary realized more than ever that this was *her* mission, *her* duty in life. And the Sioux loved her. To them she was *Wenonah*, or *Princess*, a name of honor.

In December 1885, she moved north to Little Eagle Station on the Grand River (in present South Dakota) at the Standing Rock Reservation. Her headquarters became a "square, frame cottage" about ten miles from Sitting Bull's home. Her mission covered an area eighty miles long and forty miles wide.

Sitting Bull showed up at Mary Collins' house not long after she arrived. Together they discussed her mission among his people. She would teach the children to read and write, she told him. He liked that. He was particularly pleased that she was a medicine woman.

He hoped, though, that she would not interfere with the customs and dances of his people.

Collins liked Sitting Bull, too. She detected "some very indefinable power which could not be resisted by his own people or even others who came in contact with him." He was "always so tender, gracious and invariably sweet," she wrote.

Sitting Bull and his people had lived near Little Eagle for two years. They liked Mary because she knew them and had "a working knowledge of the language." She remembered, "As a Medicine woman; I was welcomed among them. As with the Indians the Medicine man and the High Priest are one, it was not hard for them to accept me as a religious teacher also." So Mary Collins came to Sitting Bull's people as a preacher, teacher, medicine woman, and social worker.

But Collins did not limit her horizons. During the winter of 1886, she toured Ohio, Washington, D.C., and the Boston area, fulfilling speaking engagements over 29 consecutive days.

Dedicated to the Indian cause, she wrote material for the Dakota Mission paper, *Iapi Oaye (The Word Carrier)*, a monthly publication. She complained when a young man was arrested for drinking whiskey: "Ten or fifteen years in the Penitentiary would help those white men who bring whiskey on the Reservation."

At the request of the U.S. Indian Commissioner, she wrote, "Practical Suggestions on Indian Affairs." Critical of the poor choice of interpreters and doctors sent by the government among the Indians, she warned, "We must place before him (the Indian) as his teachers our best men and women if we would have a high type of manhood develop."

She opposed the government's 1887 order to change school instruction from the Sioux language to English. That same year, she wrote of the government dole: "Twenty more years of beggards with no sense of shame. They are hungry."

On July 22, 1891, Collins was appointed and commissioned postmaster at Oahe. On October 30, 1899, she was formally ordained a minister in the Congregational Church. Her ordination carried with it the duties of superintendent of the Standing Rock Mission Field.

After leaving the Dakotas, she was forced into retirement by poor health. She joined a sister in Keokuk and spoke often for the American Missionary Association. For a while during 1919, Mary served as minister of her home church, the First Congregational Church in Keokuk. That summer she became ill but enjoyed a brief recovery in the fall. Following a relapse she was bed-ridden until her death on Tuesday, May 25, 1920. She was buried in Keokuk.

The Rev. Mary Clementine Collins in later years.
(Courtesy of South Dakota State Historical Society.)

The Reverend Mary Clementine Collins, who parleyed as an equal with the legendary Sitting Bull, was respected by the Sioux because of her courage, admired by them because she taught self-sufficiency, and loved by them because she believed in them. She once wrote, "I plead for these people. They are Americans with American ancestry. They have the true American pride of country."

Statements like this made Mary Clementine Collins unusual in a day when whites did not normally view Indians from the point of view of the Indian. She was a great lady, living among a magnificent people in a remarkable time. She served her God, the Sioux, and her country well.

11

Carry Nation and Hatchetation[*]

The big woman walked down the street, taking long strides, her black alpaca dress swaying from side to side as she brushed past the startled farmers on the sidewalk. Her poke bonnet covered her iron-grey hair and shaded her small, close-set eyes from the late summer sun in Medicine Lodge, Kansas. Those who looked past her spectacles and into her black eyes saw determination.

Carry Amelia Moore Gloyd Nation was determined. And at six-feet and 175 pounds, she was tough to stop when she was on a mission. On this date in 1899, she was nearing the site of her first assault on a saloon, a "joint," as she liked to call it.

Mrs. Wesley Cain, the Medicine Lodge Baptist minister's wife, was along. They had formed a chapter of the Women's Christian Temperance Union in the mid-1890s and Carry Nation was the Jail Evangelist. And what got these prisoners into jail in the first place? Too often for Carry, the answer came back: Booze!

[*]**Hatchetation** noun: the act of using a short-handled ax to break up joints.

Carry Amelia Nation.
(Author's collection)

Now it was time to do something, to take some strong action against these illegal joints. The prohibition of the sale of intoxicating beverages was a centuries-old cause, begun, some claim, as far back as in ancient China. The Aztecs of Mexico tried it and so did inhabitants of feudal Japan.

As early as the 1780s, Dr. Benjamin Rush warned that alcoholic beverages were not good for one's health. Sylvester Graham (of Graham cracker fame) spoke against alcohol for the same reason. And by the 1830s, social and moral arguments led evangelical reformers to take up the cause.

Massachusetts experimented with a prohibition law in 1838. Called the Fifteen Gallon Law, it prohibited the sale of whiskey in quantities smaller than 15 gallons. The law was repealed two years later. (It was in Rockport, Massachusetts, in 1856, where 300 women wrecked 13 saloons.)

And there were other states that battled "demon rum." In 1845, New York allowed local governments to prohibit the manufacture and sale of alcohol. It was the next year, when Maine became the first to pass a statewide prohibition law (repealed in 1868). And by 1860, 13 of the 33 states were dry.

In 1869, the Prohibition Party was founded in the United States. Just over two decades later, the party made its best showing in the Election of 1892 when Gen. John Bidwell garnered 271,000 votes for U.S. President out of the 12,000,000 cast. And in 1893, the Anti-Saloon League was formed.

As to Carry Nation's interest in all this, while she was in her early 20s, her alcoholic husband died, leaving her widowed and with a small daughter. While not actively opposing alcoholic beverages in the early years, some say she became outraged at a U.S. Supreme Court decision in 1890 which favored the importation and sale of liquor in "original packages" from state to state, making these transactions subject only to interstate commerce laws. This decision seriously weakened the prohibition laws of Kansas.

Just now, she had immediate business and Mart Strong's saloon was her target. In front of Strong's, she turned to the crowd of onlookers, jabbed at the sky with a closed umbrella and proclaimed, "Men and women of Medicine Lodge, this is a joint! Let us pray!"

Moments later, she laid the umbrella over her shoulder, spun on her heels and pushed through the swinging doors into Strong's establishment.

Strong was ready. He heard the commotion and intercepted Carry in the front room, spun her around and shoved her out the door, all the time shouting, "Get out of here, you crazy woman!"

A few minutes later, Carry tried again. This time, Strong shoved her so violently that she landed hard on her rear end.

In the meantime, hearing the commotion, Town Marshal James Gano had come up. He saw Carry fall and he admonished Strong, "Now, Mart! Go easy, Mart!" And when Strong shoved her again after she stood up, Gano caught her.

Instead of thanking Marshal Gano, however, Carry turned on him, insisting that he do his job. Suddenly, all the women with Carry turned on Gano. Recognizing a bad situation, Gano fled down a nearby alley. And while Gano escaped, Strong slammed and locked his doors.

The women, perhaps 200 of them by now, marched directly to the Medicine Lodge mayor's home, demanding that Strong's joint be closed. Carry found out the next morning that, for whatever reason, Matt Strong had left Medicine Lodge. She had been successful.

Kansas law, because of an 1880 constitutional amendment, prohibited the sale of intoxicating beverages except for medical, scientific or mechanical purposes. The Murray Enforcement Act was upheld by the State Supreme Court in 1883, so there was no reason to believe that saloons should be operating in Medicine Lodge or anywhere else in Kansas. But it was not so.

Drugstores sold illegal beverages, doctors prescribed alcohol, and saloons, operating like the speakeasies of the 1920s, were everywhere. Drinkers and brewers paid off the necessary officials to keep the booze flowing in Kansas, even threatening to overturn the amendment of 1880 responsible for making Kansas a "dry" state in the first place.

Now, in 1899, Carry planned on doing something about all that. She figured that before Mart Strong left, there were seven joints in Medicine Lodge. That meant there were six more joints to close. Next on the women's list was a joint run by Harry Durst.

Carry and the women marched to Durst's place and dropped to their knees to begin praying at the top of their voices. Those inside, hearing this, scattered in all directions, leaving Durst alone to face the women's wrath.

Durst came out and Carry grabbed him, screaming that he was headed for hell. More concerned at this time about Carry than hell, Durst escaped inside, but Carry continued yelling that she was going to close his joint.

Durst fled Medicine Lodge and Kansas.

In early 1900, she closed down Hank O'Bryan's. Three weeks later, three more joints were closed by city officials. A druggist, O.L. Day, skipped out of town a few weeks later. Medicine Lodge was drying up.

But these victories had their price. Carry's home was vandalized. Broken windows and the threat of being burned out were common. On one occasion, someone cut her horse's harness and the buggy she rode in was wrecked. City officials, however, began looking on her favorably. Not long after, she was elected president of the Barber County WCTU. Carry Nation was finally admired.

"Admired" is one of the things that Carry Nation was. But she was many other things in her lifetime. In 1909, when she penned her autobiography, *The Use and Need of the Life of Carry A. Nation,* she signed it, "Your loving Home Defender." (The book was dedicated to the Women's Christian Temperance Union.) Some called her simply, "Mother Nation." And when a temperance organization in Kansas gave her a medal, it was enscribed: "The Bravest Woman in Kansas."

Carry admired one description that likened her to "a bulldog running along at the feet of Jesus, barking at what He doesn't like." One newspaper praised her, saying that she was a "woman of simple character, with an unerring instinct for the moral law." Others called her: "Carry Nation, Joint Smasher"; or "The Lady with the Hatchet"; or "The Commander-in-Chief, the Hatchet Army."

But if there were kind descriptions, there were cruel ones. One writer said that she was a "village nuisance" who turned into a "national affliction." Another referred to her as "that crazy woman from Kansas." And still another claimed that "her tongue was hinged in the middle and loose at both ends."

Biographer Herbert Asbury called her "the most industrious meddler and busy-body that even the Middle West, hot-bed of the bizarre and the fanatical, has ever produced."

Carry Amelia Moore was born to George Moore and the former Mary Campbell Caldwell on the Dix River in Garrard County, Kentucky, on November 25, 1846. George Moore was a stock trader and a slaveholder. Carry's mother had been married before to a man named Will Caldwell, who died in Sangamon County, Illinois. The George Moore house where Carry was born was a 10-room, hewed-log house that was weatherboarded and plastered.

The Moores moved to near Danville, Kentucky, in Boyle County, shortly after 1850. Carry attended her first school following the family's next move to Woodford County, between Midway and Versailles, Kentucky. (Carry later attended the following Missouri schools: Mrs. Tillery's boarding school in Independence, a boarding school at Liberty, and the State Normal School at Warrensburg.)

By 1855, the Moores lived in Belton, Missouri, in Cass County. From there, Carry attended the Christian Church at Hickman's Mill, just across the line in Jackson County. She was converted and baptized there. (Her religious upbringing was also influenced by a spiritualist sect that came to Cass County shortly after the Civil War. A Mrs. Jane Hawkins headed this group, and Carry's father helped Hawkins locate in nearby Peculiar, Missouri.)

During these years, Carry had digestive disorders that left her a semi-invalid. By 1861, however, the Moores were on the move again. These were volatile times for people living in northwest Missouri because of the guerilla warfare taking place back and forth across the Kansas border. George Moore decided to try his luck in Texas.

Moore's ox-drawn wagon train rolled out of Belton with the Moore family riding in an elegant carriage, headed for Grayson County, Texas, north of Dallas. They herded their mules, horses and cattle on a trek that took six weeks. Once in Texas, bad luck found them again. Some of their mules and horses died, and typhoid fever swept away many of Moore's slaves. He lost nearly everything, so he sold out, slaves and all, and prepared to return north.

The elegant carriage the Moore family rode to Texas was traded for provisions and bedding for the return trip. On their return trip to Missouri, they ran into the war. At Pea Ridge in northwest Arkansas, Gen. Sam Curtis (USA) and Gen. Earl Van Dorn (CSA) tangled in March, 1862. The Moores turned over some of their pillows and blankets to the Confederate wounded from Pea Ridge, then continued their journey north.

During 1862 and 1863, in Cass County, conditions grew more volatile. And after Confederate guerilla leader, Col. William C. Quantrill, raided Lawrence, Kansas, killing about 150 men and boys, Senator James Lane of Kansas insisted that harsh measures be taken against Confederate sympathizers. As a result, "General Orders No. 11, Missouri" were issued and residents of Jackson,

Bates and half of Vernon counties, Missouri, were forced to move. In Cass County, where the Moores lived, 9,400 of the 10,000 residents were forced to move. This was considered by many the most severe military act of the war against civilians. George Moore took a job in Kansas City and worked there until the war ended.

Carry adored her father. She wrote once, "If I ever had an angel on earth, it was my father. He was not a saint, but a man—one of the noblest works of God."

Her mother was ill during much of the Civil War, so Carry took over the household. Often deranged, Mary Moore sometimes claimed she was the reigning monarch of England, Queen Victoria. She was admitted to the State Hospital at Nevada, Missouri, on August 12, 1890, and died there September 14, 1893. Carry said that heart disease killed her mother; hospital records reveal that Mary Moore suffered from "recurrent mania" and that her mother, brother and sister all were mentally ill.

Somewhere in the years before and during the Civil War, Carry began thinking of marriage. Some said she was "prim, prissy and suspicious" of men in her young life. Carry wrote, "I had been taught that to inspire respect and love from a man you must keep him at a distance." She added that she looked for "the qualities of the mind."

Shortly after the Civil War, a young doctor and Civil War veteran, Dr. Charles Gloyd, from Newport, Ohio, and his mother arrived in Belton. George Moore helped Gloyd find a teaching job at a country school, and Gloyd and his mother roomed at the Moores. Highly educated, Dr. Gloyd spoke several languages, no doubt impressing Carry.

Dr. Gloyd apparently also admired Carry's qualities because, one day, as they passed in a darkened hallway, Gloyd grasped her hand and kissed her. Carry could only gasp and cry out, "I am ruined, I am ruined."

In the months that followed, Dr. Gloyd's intentions were revealed as honorable, and he asked for her hand in marriage. Eventually, Gloyd left the Moore home in Belton to set up a medical practice in

Holden, Missouri. Carry's parents had picked out a prosperous young farmer for Carry to marry. Besides, Gloyd, formerly a captain in the 118th Ohio Volunteers, was a hard drinker, a fact her father warned her about.

Ignoring all of this, Gloyd and Carry were married in Belton on November 21, 1867. They made their home in Holden, but life was no honeymoon. Over the next months, Gloyd's practice suffered, and his bride became pregnant. Often, Holden residents could see this tall, pregnant, distraught young woman trodding the streets searching for her drunken husband and, too often, finding that he had escaped into the confines of the hated Masonic Lodge, where she was not allowed to enter. She wrote, "He seemed to want to be away from me."

In a short time, Carry came to despise alcohol, fraternal organizations and tobacco. "The world was like a place of torture," she remembered of that time.

By the summer of 1868, she was on the verge of a nervous breakdown, and her father took her home. From Belton, she appealed to her husband to stop drinking. He visited her, but Carry's mother let it be known that Dr. Gloyd was not welcome. Carry's daughter, Charlien, was born later in the year, but six weeks passed before Carry informed Gloyd that he was a father. Then, just six months after the birth of Charlien, Carry got word that she was a widow. Dr. Gloyd was dead. She collapsed. (She wrote later, he was the "man I loved more than my own life.")

The widowed Carry and her daughter moved to Holden to try to make a living on rental property left by her deceased husband. Failing at that and with the help of friends, she attended the State Normal School at Warrensburg (now Central Missouri State University). With a teacher's certificate, she returned to Holden to teach the primary grades in the public school.

For four years, Carry taught, but in the mid-1870s, one of the school board members criticized the way she taught pronunciation. She was fired. The board member's niece got her job. (Others add that she taught a strange form of calligraphy to her students and did not follow the rules well.)

With no other jobs available, Carry resolved, out of desperation, that her only hope was to remarry. Ten days later, the editor of the *Warrensburg Journal* newspaper came to Holden. Nineteen years older than Carry, David Nation was a handsome man with flowing whiskers. He also was a minister and had studied law. They began their life together the summer of 1877. It was a marriage filled with bickering and unhappiness, but it lasted for 24 years.

During 1879, David and Carry Nation traded their Missouri property for 1,700 acres on the San Bernard River in Brazoria County, Texas. Not unlike Carry's 1860s experience in Texas, this time, fate also dealt blow after blow to Carry and her family. Their horses were soon dead. A neighbor threw their farming equipment in the river. And a farmhand stole what little money they had.

Nation took his legal training and moved to Columbia, 50 miles from Houston to begin a law practice, leaving Carry, Charlien and Nation's daughter, Lola, behind on the farm. (Dr. Gloyd's mother, Mrs. Gloyd, also lived with the Nation family.)

There was little food and less money, and before long, Carry loaded everyone into a buckboard and followed her husband to Columbia. There, she took over the Columbia Hotel and became the sole support of the family, toiling long hours to make a success of the hotel, all the time growing more and more bitter at the life fate had dealt her. It was while Carry lived in Columbia that she had the first indications that her daughter, Charlien, was "afflicted," a problem that Carry blamed on Gloyd's drunkenness. (Charlien later suffered from a huge sore that ate away the cheek, exposing her teeth. She also had locked jaws that doctors in Houston, San Antonio, New York and Philadelphia could not cure.)

In 1881, the family moved again, this time to Richmond in Fort Bend County, Texas. They did better there, but medical expenses for Charlien ravaged their income. Carry increasingly suffered from nervousness, insomnia and depression.

Then, during 1884, the Methodists held a conference and revival in Richmond. Carry, desperate and looking for a way to save herself, attended all the sessions. Her religious fervor became so radical that many felt she was losing her mind. She now claimed that she had visions.

David Nation would later talk of this period as the breaking point for him. He claimed he could not bear her extremism. And Carry would counter: "My Christian life was an offence unto him."

By 1888, Lola Nation, Carry's step-daughter, and Charlien had both married. Charlien's husband was Alexander McNabb of Richmond, Texas. During 1904, Charlien was judged insane and committed to the State Lunatic Asylum at Austin, Texas. Carry had her dismissed but sent her to Oklahoma and then to Maryland, where on June 11, 1907, she was placed in the Richard Gundry Home at Catonsville near Baltimore. She was suffering from "chronic mania" but was discharged on November 25, 1910. Alcoholism was a part of Charlien's problem.

In 1889, David and Carry Nation sold out in Texas and moved to Kansas where he became a minister in the Christian Church. They were in Holton, north of Topeka, for a time, but finally settled on Medicine Lodge Creek in the town of Medicine Lodge.

Carry enjoyed being a minister's wife. She wrote and edited some of Nation's sermons, especially those attacking alcohol, tobacco and local problems. Every sermon found her in the front pew prompting her husband. Whenever she felt that he was boring his congregation, she would rise, step into the aisle and call out, "That will be about all for today, David!"

At Medicine Lodge, Nation resumed practicing law and Carry and David settled into a brick home at present 211 West Fowler Avenue. It was in Medicine Lodge that she increasingly became a crusading busybody. She snatched cigarettes from the mouths of smokers. She admonished women whose skirts were not long enough. She stopped young couples on the street and warned the young man to act toward the girl "as he would toward his sister."

Sometimes, she reminded the young woman that men were like vultures.

But her list of people and things to condemn did not end there. She disliked corsets, too. And well-dressed women were "mannikins hung with the filthy rags of fashion." Men who belonged to clubs were "diamond-studded, gold-fobbed rummies whose bodies are reeking masses of corruption." And in the same breath, she could protest foreign foods and "mildly pornographic art."

Nothing, it seemed, was safe from her fired-up tongue. Policemen, according to Carry, were "rum-soaked, whiskey-swilled, saturn-faced rummies." William Jennings Bryan, a candidate for U.S. President three times during Carry's lifetime, was "for Bryan and what Bryan could get for Bryan." After President William McKinley was assassinated, she pointed out that he might have recovered "had not his blood been poisoned by nicotine." She called President Theodore Roosevelt "blood-thirsty, reckless, and a cigarette-smoking rummy." As for government, she proclaimed, it is "like a dead fish, stinks worse at the head." She could, indeed, be a busybody.

When Carry attended church, she sometimes asked for the preacher's credentials. She liked to point out that Christ had appeared to her and told her he did not drink wine, but grape juice. Local merchants became upset with her when she asked them for donations for the poor. To men of wealth, she proclaimed, "The time is coming when the millionaire will be the despised of all people. I wish for the poor often to make the rich take back seats." And when she met a whiskey seller on the street, she greeted him, her shrill voice, loud and clear, "Good morning, destroyer of men's souls!" At other times, she screeched, "Good morning, maker of drunkards and widows!"

Following the 1899 raid on Mart Strong's joint and the 1900 raids in Medicine Lodge, Carry Nation was determined to continue her fight for the enforcement of Kansas law. In the spring, she invaded Kiowa, Kansas, a Barber County community along the Oklahoma border where bootlegging was rampant. She accused the county attorney there of taking bribes. He denied it and sued her for slander. She lost the case, but appealed to the Kansas attorney general and governor. Nothing was done about closing the joints by these officials, so she decided to smash them as she had done in Medicine Lodge.

She wrote of this time, "I felt desperate. I felt that I had rather die than see saloons come back to Kansas." She took her Bible in hand, prayed and resolved, "There is to be a change in my life!" From that day, June 5, 1900, her life was devoted solely, it seemed, to her mission.

Finally, she hitched up her horse, Prince, and drove her buggy the 20 miles or so to Kiowa and directly to Dobson's saloon. Armed with bricks and stones, she entered and told Dobson, "I am going to break up this den of vice." She then sang a hymn or two and made good her word by hurling bricks. The joint wrecked, Carry called out, "Now Mr. Dobson, I have finished. God be with you."

Lewis' saloon was next. She was developing a routine. She entered, sang, prayed and tongue-lashed the drinkers. (Religious hymns were often sung, but she also liked "The Campbells Are Coming!" in honor of her mother's father, James Campbell, whose parents were from Scotland.) To the owner, she often directed Biblical quotations. Then she began smashing the joint.

Following the Lewis smashing, there was some talk about her paying for the broken windows, but she told the marshal and mayor she would not pay since these were the trappings of hell she was destroying. There was no law against that, she figured. They told her to go home.

Back in Medicine Lodge, Carry was greeted as a heroine by the local WCTU. (The state WCTU made sure Carry denied any connection with them and her raid on Kiowa.) Word came that not only had Carry smashed Kiowa joints, but a tornado had struck several Kansas towns that had joints. Over the next days, newspapers picked up the Kiowa raid news and letters began pouring in from all over Kansas, encouraging her even more. In a short time, Barber County was rid of saloons for the first time, an achievement that law enforcement officials had not been able to accomplish in two decades.

Carry began sizing up Wichita, a community of about 25,000 Kansans and 40 or 50 saloons. It was December, 1900, two days after Christmas, when she stepped off the train there and attacked the saloon in the basement of the Hotel Carey.

She stepped through the door into the hotel's saloon, surveyed the elegant, curved bar, glanced at the $1,500 plateglass mirror behind it and the huge oil painting on the opposite wall, and announced, "Glory to God! Peace on earth, good will to men!"

One of her first rocks shattered the glass-covered picture of the naked "Cleopatra at the Bath," scattering the early morning drinkers at the cherry-wood bar. The $1,500 mirror was next. She then pulled an iron rod and a cane from her skirts and began slashing out at anything in striking distance.

When the Wichita police finally arrived, she was still smashing. Bottles were broken and tables overturned. A shiny, brass spittoon was overturned and dented. A Detective Massey told her, "Madam, I must arrest you for defacing property."

She spun and screamed, the veins on her neck about to pop, "Defacing? I am defacing nothing! I am destroying!"

She was taken to the Sedgwick County Jail to await a January 5, 1901 trial. She warned, "You put me in here a cub, but I will go out a roaring lion and make all hell howl." And she continued to spread the word from jail. A visiting delegation of women was told, "Take your consecrated hatchets, rocks and brick-bats and everything that comes handy, and you can clean this curse out! Don't wait for the ballots! Smash! Smash!"

Now, not only Kansas was stirred up by this woman, but she was gaining national attention. Congratulatory letters and telegrams kept her busy in jail. Finally, in mid-January, 1901, she was released from jail. A crowd jammed the streets to greet the freed Carry. She screamed to them, "Show me a joint!"

David Nation quickly intervened and convinced her to retire to Newton for a short rest.

January 21, 1901, was a Monday. And it was the day that Carry Nation returned to Wichita. By now, she wore what had become a sort of black-and-white, clerical-looking uniform, a long black dress with a white scarf around her neck. Following a meeting of the Wichita chapter of the WCTU, Carry, with hatchet in hand, led a parade of armed women into the streets. At first, they attracted little attention. In low, quiet voices, they sang "Onward Christian Soldiers." Then, as they turned into Douglas Avenue, there stood James Burnes' saloon.

Carry led the ladies through the doors and the bar-sitters scattered in all directions. The bartender came around the bar, his arms out, pleading in a calm, soothing voice, "Now, ladies."

Carry, her head tilted down and the black eyes staring from under bushy eyebrows, yelled, "Don't come near my hatchet! It might fall on you, and I will not be responsible for the results!"

Carry's hatchet-filled hand flashed, the shiny blade whistling by the bartender's ear. He jumped back as she ordered, "Out of my way, you rummy!"

That was enough excitement for him; he fled to the back of the room and hid behind a table, watching as she called out, "Smash, women! Smash!"

Fifteen minutes later, the job done, Carry stood in the center of the room, surveyed the damage and proclaimed, "Peace on earth, good will to men!"

"Praise God!" her fellow smashers intoned.

Carry stepped through the door, pushing by James Burnes, the owner. "God be with you!" she said to him.

John Herrig's Palace Cafe was next on Carry's list, but Herrig did not take kindly to her invasion and placed a pistol to her head and told her he planned to blow her brains out. She retreated but warned that God would certainly strike him dead.

Fearing a riot, Wichita police intercepted the women and herded them to police headquarters. Before Carry entered, she climbed onto a wagon, quieted the crowd, held her fist in the air and called out, "Men of Wichita, this is the right arm of God! I am destined to wreck every saloon in your city!" Wichita would never be the same.

In the next days and weeks, Wichita reeled from the effects of her visit. Insurance companies cancelled the policies of the joints, and bar owners hired guards. When a group organized to close the joints in late January, the saloonkeepers had to hire still more guards.

Carry's next target was Enterprise, six miles from Abilene in Dickinson County. John Schilling and William Shook owned saloons, but she found both closed. She rattled Shilling's door and shouted, "Open this door, you rummy! This is God's work!"

When no one answered, she began slashing at the door with her hatchet. The town marshal stopped her. He made it clear that he would use force if she continued.

After a meal at a friend's home, she returned to town to a street corner in speak. She was just getting warmed to the task, and about five minutes into her speech, when John Schilling's wife arrived on the scene. She walked up to Carry, fire in her eyes, and began pummeling her in the face. Mrs. Schilling bruised one of Carry's eyes and left a deep gash over the other.

When Carry recovered, she chased Mrs. Schilling but failed to catch her. Someone offered her a beefsteak. Carry covered the bruised eye and finished her speech.

The next morning, Carry and about 50 women visited Shook's but did not attack his place, just warned him. They then headed for Schilling's, where they were met by a gang of town toughs, all determined to stop Carry. Words and rotten eggs were hurled, staggering Carry, who dropped her hatchet. That gave Mrs. Schilling and her friends a chance to beat Carry to the ground with whips and sticks. Finally, after an older woman came to Carry's defense, Carry's backers rallied and drove off Mrs. Schilling's group. All were arrested and most were fined for this public outburst.

A few days later, Carry was in Topeka, the Kansas capital. It was a crusader's delight. There were 40 joints in the city, but no saloons operating in the open. At Edward Myers' Cigar Store, Mrs. Myers met her with a broom, slapped Carry on the head and the rear, then chased her down the street.

When Mrs. Myers abandoned the chase, Carry checked out a chili parlor and found it in order. But when she exited the parlor, she faced a belligerent mob and had to flee to the State Capitol building. Finally safe, she announced, "Hell seems to be howling tonight!" Thus ended her first day in Topeka.

With the assistance of students from Washburn College, Carry put Topeka on edge over the next few days. There were threats against her. In addition, the Missouri Brewers' Association sent $600 to help buy more guards for the Topeka joints. And on February 4, Carry bought six new hatchets at the Topeka Cash Store. Edward Murphy's Unique Restaurant drew her attention, but she was shoved and kicked by guards there and finally rescued by two policemen.

Carry then entered a hardware store and bought 30 hatchets to pass out to the ladies who accompanied her. Finally, they attacked the Senate Bar, their slashing, smashing hatchetation leaving the bar a shambles. She was arrested again, but all charges were dropped since there was no law against breaking up joints. (It was in Topeka that Carry began selling tiny, souvenir hatchets, making a good profit from them at 25 or 50 cents each.)

She addressed the Kansas legislature, but a law introduced the next day to legalize saloon smashing failed to pass. The newspapers were, of course, carrying the word about Carry and before long, she was hired to speak outside Kansas.

A.C. Rankin, a professional temperance lecturer, booked her for a tour that took her through Iowa and to Chicago, before returning to Topeka later in February. She was jailed almost immediately, but issued a plea from jail: "Organize, home defenders, and jump for the hatchet, and run to the dive and smash the murder shop. Delay only means more souls in hell; more girls in houses of prostitution; more naked children; more crushed hearts and homes; more devils; more hell; less of virtue, more of vice, less of heaven, less of life and more of death." Two days later, Carry began a publishing project. *The Smasher's Mail* appeared on Topeka streets on February 21.

By late February, she was out of jail and in Peoria, Illinois, where she spoke in the Opera House. She reminded her audience that Peoria made more rye whiskey than any city in the world. They did not pay her the full $150 speaking fee.

In March, she was in and out of jail in Topeka and Kansas City. In Topeka, she had a peace bond that forced her to steer clear of the joints, and she noticed the townspeople seemed tired of her.

But she had other business to take care of. A National Hatchet Brigade had formed, and Carry Nation Clubs were springing up. Newspapers across the country were describing her exploits on their front pages.

Carry was commended by the French Women's Christian Temperance Society, and in Concord, Nebraska, elected city officials pledged to confer with Carry in all matters. Instead of playing "Cowboys and Indians," children played "Smasher."

Bartenders named drinks after her, while bars around the country were taking the name, the "Carry Nation Bar." One saloon had a sign: "All Nations Welcome But Carry!"

Over the next months, she traveled, carrying her familiar black satchel loaded with the souvenir, miniature hatchets, Home Defender buttons and *The Smasher's Mail*, all of them for sale.

In St. Louis' Union Station, she stepped down from a train and scolded smokers, knocking cigars and cigarettes from the mouths of astonished men as she screeched, "I want all you hellions to quit puffing that hell-fume into God's clean air!"

She heard about Joseph Sauerburger's "Carry Nation Bar" near Union Station at 16th and Market and threatened him, saying, "I'll use a little hatchetation on you!" But when she returned a short time later to make good her word, Sauerburger ran her out of his place with a pistol. (Carry admitted that she hoped her death would be violent. She felt the Lord had chosen her to be a martyr. When told that another saloonkeeper planned to shoot her, she responded, "O, I want to be shot! How glorious to be a Martyr to the cause.")

Later that year, she worked for James E. Furlong, head of the Furlong Lyceum Bureau of Rochester, New York. She spoke first in Clarksburg, Ohio, and then across the country, lecturing in Carnegie Hall and shouting insults at saloons in New York City and on Coney Island. In front of one saloon, she screamed, "How many souls have been murdered in this drunkard factory today?"

Always, she remained the busybody, the meddler. In Buffalo, New York, for example, she confronted a priest who was smoking, "What a shame for a man to dress like a saint and to smell like a devil!" It was just her nature. She admitted, "I never saw anything that needed rebuke, exhortation or warning but that I felt it was my duty to meddle with it."

Carry returned to Medicine Lodge in November for the first time in nearly a year. She had received word in August that David Nation had sued her for divorce on grounds of "cruelty & desertion." He added that she had taken his featherbed and some money out of his checking account. She said the featherbed was hers and that she planned to fight the divorce in order to get her share of his pension money. The divorce was granted in November, but only on grounds of desertion. Their property was divided equally, but Carry got none of the pension.

Nation took a parcel of land, and she got their house in Medicine Lodge. She sold the house a year later for $800. She said of Nation, "David isn't a bad fellow, but he is too slow for me." On another occasion, she commented, "My Christian life was an offence unto him." When he died two years later, she simply said, "I shall meet him on that day when the secrets of all hearts shall be made manifest."

In the next years, she wrote her autobiography and a temperance play ("The War on Drink), did some acting, and established a

"Home for Drunkards' Wives and Mothers." She spoke on college campuses and bought the Harvest Home Mission in Guthrie, Oklahoma. In the meantime, she continued smashing joints and taking abuse.

In Nebraska City, a bartender punched her. An Elizabethtown, Kentucky saloonkeeper broke a chair over her head. At Trinidad, Colorado, she was thrown so hard out of a saloon that she swallowed her false teeth, coughed them up and broke them. And she was even muscled out of May Maloy's Dance Hall and Cafe in Butte, Montana by May Maloy.

In 1907, she was given five-year use of a furnished apartment at 217 D Street in Washington, D.C. She announced that the nation's capitol would be her home.

Carry Nation's remaining years were not unlike her early hatchetation days in 1900 and 1901. Armed with her trusty hatchets (Faith, Hope and Charity), she continued to terrorize joints wherever she went. She was arrested in cities throughout the United States, Canada and the British Isles. Washington, D.C., alone, slapped her in jail seven times. One of her last arrests came in Pittsburgh. She verbally attacked a man wearing a Masonic pin, one like her first husband, Dr. Charles Gloyd, had worn.

One interviewer who caught up with her in these later years wrote that Carry

Carry Nation onboard ship, headed for Europe.
(Author's collection)

was a "queer, frowzy, fat, unromantic Joan of Arc who heard voices and saw visions, and who made no move unless she was spiritually guided."

Carry's strength and health were failing and she returned to her cottage in Alpena Pass (Boone County), Arkansas. She spoke at Eureka Springs (Carroll County) near the Missouri border on January 13, 1911, just 10 years after those first, rousing, crusading days in Wichita. At age 64, her words still came evenly, her shrill voice clear and ringing in the hall. Then, something changed. She seemed to lose her chain of thought. Confusion swept her face. Finally, in a slow, deliberate whisper, she concluded, "I, I have done what I could."

She collapsed.

Carry Nation was admitted to the Evergreen Hospital in Leavenworth, Kansas the next day. She was apathetic and listless; her mind seemed to fail. Over the next months, not much changed. Finally, on June 9, she passed away. The hospital said she died of "nervous trouble due to her unusual activities causing a weakening of the heart."

Carry was buried beside her mother in Belton Cemetery, Belton, Missouri. The gravesite was left unmarked until May 30, 1924, when the Carry Nation Monument Association erected a granite shaft. The monument reads:

CARRY A. NATION
Faithful to the Cause of Prohibition
"She Hath Done What She Could"

Aftermath

The climate of public opinion that Carry Nation helped establish and left behind influenced the prohibition movement over the next decade. On January 16, 1920, the 18th Amendment to prohibit the sale, manufacture or transportation of intoxicating beverages went into effect throughout the United States, enforced by the Volstead Act of October 28, 1919.

For many reasons, by 1933, Americans were no longer interested in prohibition, and on December 5 of that year, the state of Utah became the 36th state to approve the 21st Amendment to the U.S. Constitution, an amendment that repealed prohibition.

By 1966, all states had abandoned prohibition, although some local areas continue to have prohibition.

As to Carry Nation, her influence continues to be felt. Interestingly enough, as late as 1988, a national WCTU spokesperson complained, "Carry Nation is our biggest menace. We got stuck with her image."

CARRY NATION'S FOUR RULES FOR LONGEVITY

1. If you would live long, walk by twenty saloons a day.
2. If you must pour liquor, pour it down the sewer.
3. Do not chew tobacco unless you prefer to take your food predigested after forty.
4. Drink all the water you want whenever you want it.

Bibliography

Annual Report of the Association of Graduates. Obituary: Fayette Roe. June 12, 1917. West Point, NY. 71.

Asbury, Herbert. *Carry Nation: The Woman with the Hatchet*. New York, NY: Alfred A. Knopf, 1929.

Bartholomew, Ed. *Wyatt Earp: The Man and the Myth*. Toyahvale, TX: Frontier Book Company, 1964.

Black Hills Daily Times. December 7, 8, 10, 1877.

Borst, John C. "Dakota Resources: The Marcy C. Collins Family Papers at the South Dakota Historical Resource Center," *South Dakota History*. Vol. 12, No. 4, Winter 1982. 248-253.

Boyer, Glenn G. *The Suppressed Murder of Wyatt Earp*. San Antonio, TX: The Naylor Company, 1967.

Bowman III, Mrs. Joseph. "A Letter: Franklin (TN) County Historian to Larry D. Underwood," November 23, 1988.

Brown, Dee. *The Fetterman Massacre*. Lincoln, NE: University of Nebraska Press, 1971.

———. *The Galvanized Yankees*. New York, NY: Curtis Books, 1963.

Carrington, Frances. *My Army Life*. Philadelphia, PA: J.B. Lippincott & Co., 1911.

Carter, Capt. R.G. *On the Border with Mackenzie*. New York, NY: Antiquarian Press, Ltd., 1961.

Cheyenne *Daily Leader*, October 29, 30, 31, 1879.

Clum, John Philip. *It All Happened in Tombstone*. Flagstaff, AZ: Northland Press, 1965.

Collins, Mary C. "An Experience," *Iapi Oapi*. Vol. IX, No. 8, August 1880.

——. "Winona: The Autobiography of Rev. Mary C. Collins," (Pamphlet). American Missionary Association, New York, NY. 1918.

Coroner's Inquest, November 1, 1879, in the matter of the shooting of Edward Malone. Wyoming State Archives and Historical Department.

Dary, David. *True Tales of the Old-Time Plains*. New York, NY: Crown Publishers, Inc., 1979.

DeShields, James T. *Border Wars of Texas*. Tioga, TX: The Herald Co., 1912.

Drago, Harry Sinclair. *Roads to Empire*. New York, NY: Dodd, Mead & Co., 1968.

Earp, Josephine Sarah Marcus. *I Married Wyatt Earp*. Glenn G. Boyer, ed. Tucson, AZ: The University of Arizona Press, 1976.

Farley, Alan W. "An Indian Captivity and Its Legal Aftermath," *Kansas Historical Quarterly*. Vol. XXI, No. 4. Winter, 1954. 247-256.

Faulk, Odie B. *Tombstone: Myth and Reality*. New York, NY: Oxford University Press, 1972.

Fehrenbach, T.R. *Lone Star: A History of Texas and the Texans*. New York, NY: The MacMillan Company, 1968.

Finerty, John F. *Warpath and Bivouac*. Lincoln, NE: University of Nebraska Press, 1970.

"Fort Parker State Recreation Park" (Pamphlet), Texas Parks & Wildlife Department, Austin, TX. (no date).

Gard, Wayne. *Rawhide Texas*. Norman, OK: University of Oklahoma Press, 1965.

——. *Sam Bass*. Boston, MA & New York, NY: Houghton Mifflin Company, 1936.

Glasscock, C.B. *Lucky Baldwin*. New York, NY: A.L. Burt Company, 1933.

Hall, Carroll D., ed. *Donner Miscellany: 41 Diaries and Documents*. San Francisco, CA: The Book Club of California, 1947.

Hall, Gene. "Letters: Illiopolis (IL) historian to Larry D. Underwood," December 12, 1977 and January 15, 1978.

Hebard, Grace Raymond and E.A. Brininstool. *The Bozeman Trail.* Glendale, CA: The Arthur H. Clark Co., 1960.

Herring, Johanna R. "A Letter: Wabash College (IN) librarian to Larry D. Underwood," October 24, 1988.

Hogg, Alex. *Life and Adventures of Sam Bass.* Dallas, TX: Dallas Commercial Steam Print, 1878.

Iapi Oaye. Vol. XVII, No. 8-11. October-November 1888.

Interment Record, City of Cheyenne, WY, Cemetery Records filed in the Office of the City Clerk.

Kanamine, Linda. "Group alters style, not message," *USA Today.* August 18, 1988. 6A.

Kelly, Fanny. *Narrative of My Captivity among the Sioux Indians.* New York, NY: Corinth Books, 1962.

Leckie, Robert. *The Wars of America.* 2 volumes. New York, NY: Harper & Row, Publishers, 1968.

McGlasham, C.F. *History of the Donner Party.* Stanford, CA: Stanford University Press, 1954.

Magoffin, Susan Shelby. *Down the Santa Fe Trail and Into Mexico: The Diary of Susan Shelby Magoffin, 1846-47.* Stella M. Drumm, ed. New Haven, CT: Yale University Press, 1926.

Martin, Charles L. *A Sketch of Sam Bass, the Bandit.* Norman, OK: University of Oklahoma Press, 1956 (1880).

Martin, Douglas D. *The Earps of Tombstone.* Tombstone, AZ: Tombstone Epitaph, 1959.

Mayhall, Mildred P. *Indian Wars of Texas.* Waco, TX: Texian Press, 1965.

Murphy, Virginia Reed. "Across the Plains in the Donner Party," *Century.* Vol. XLII, 1891. 409-426.

Nevins, Allan. *Ordeal of the Union: Fruits of Manifest Destiny 1847-1852.* New York, NY: Charles Scribners Sons, 1947.

Nation, Carry A. *The Use and Need of the Life of Carry Nation.* Topeka, KS: F.M. Steves & Sons, 1909.

Notable American Women, 1607-1950. Volume 21. Cambridge, MA: Belknap Press of Harvard University Press, 1971.

Olsen, Louis P. "Mary Clementine Collins, Dacotah Missionary," *North Dakota History.* Vol. 19, No. 1, January 1952. 59-81.

O'Neal, Kathleen M. "The Sawyer Expedition," *True West,* February 1987.

Peckham, Howard H. *Captured by Indians.* New Brunswick, NJ: Rutgers University Press, 1954.

Pence, Mary Lou and Lola M. Homsher. *The Ghost Towns of Wyoming.* New York, NY: Hastings House, 1956.

Power, John Carroll. *History of the Early Settlers of Sangamon County, Illinois.* Springfield, IL, 1876.

Richardson, Rupert Norval. *The Frontier of Northwest Texas: 1846-1876.* Glendale, CA: The Arthur H. Clark Co., 1963.

Riley, Glenda. *Women and Indians on the Frontier: 1825-1915.* Albuquerque, NM: University of New Mexico Press, 1984.

Robinson, Doane. *Encyclopedia of South Dakota.* Pierre, SD: 1925.

——. "Tales of Dakota," *South Dakota Historical Collections.* Vol. XIV. 1928.

Roe, Frances M.A. *Army Letters From An Officer's Wife: 1871-1888.* Lincoln, NE: University of Nebraska Press, 1981 (1909).

Ross, Ishbel. *Charmers and Cranks.* New York, NY: Harper & Row, Publishers, 1965.

South Dakota Historical Collections. Vol. XXVIII, 1954.

South Dakota Historical Collections. Vol. XXIX, 1958.

Sowell, Andrew J. *Rangers and Pioneers of Texas.* New York, NY: Argosy-Antequarian, Ltd., 1964 (1884).

Spring, Agnes Wright. *The Cheyenne and Black Hills Stage and Express Routes.* Lincoln, NE: University of Nebraska Press, 1967.

Springfield *Illinois State Journal*, September 16, 1847 and December 16, 1847.

Steen, Ralph W., ed. *The Texas News*. Austin, TX: The Steck Company, 1955.

Stevens, Peter F. "The Proving Ground," *American History Illustrated*. Vol. XXIII, No. 3, May 1988. 38-44.

Stewart, George R. *Ordeal by Hunger: The Story of the Donner Party*. Boston, MA: Houghton Mifflin Company, 1960 (1936).

Taylor, Robert Lewis. *Vessel of Wrath: The Life and Times of Carry Nation*. New York, NY: The New American Library, Inc., 1966.

Tombstone *Daily Epitaph*, October 27, 1881.

Van Slyke, Sue C. "The Truth About the Clantons." *Quarterly of the National Association and Center for Outlaw and Lawman History*. 7 (Spring 1982) 12-16.

Vestal, Stanley, ed. *New Sources of Indian History, 1850-1891*. Norman, OK: University of Oklahoma Press, 1934.

———. *Sitting Bull, Champion of the Sioux*. Norman, OK: University of Oklahoma Press, 1957.

Wallace, Ernest and E. Adamson Hoebel. *The Comanches: Lords of the South Plains*. Norman, OK: University of Oklahoma Press, 1952.

White, E.E. *Experiences of a Special Indian Agent*. Norman, OK: University of Oklahoma Press, 1965 (Rev. ed.).

Wiltsey, Norman B. *Brave Warriors*. Caldwell, ID: The Caxton Printers, Ltd., 1963.

Wyoming: A Guide to Its History, Highways, and People (American Guide Series). New York, NY: Oxford University Press, 1941.

Yoakum, Henderson. *History of Texas*. 2 vols. New York, NY: Redfield, 1888.

Index

ORDER DIRECT 1-800-36-MEDIA

☐ YES, I want ____ copies of **Love And Glory: Women of the West** for $9.95 plus $2.50 shipping.

☐ YES, I also want ____ copies of **The Custer Fight And Other Tales of the Old West** for $9.95 plus $2.50 shipping.

Method of payment

☐ Check for $_____ to: Ship to: _____
    Media Publishing   _____
    2440 'O' Street   _____
    Suite 202   _____
    Lincoln, NE 68510

☐ Charge my credit card
    ☐ Visa   ☐ MasterCard
Account #_____
Exp. Date _____
Signature _____
Phone # _____

ORDER DIRECT 1-800-36-MEDIA

☐ YES, I want ____ copies of **Love And Glory: Women of the West** for $9.95 plus $2.50 shipping.

☐ YES, I also want ____ copies of **The Custer Fight And Other Tales of the Old West** for $9.95 plus $2.50 shipping.

Method of payment

☐ Check for $_____ to: Ship to: _____
    Media Publishing   _____
    2440 'O' Street   _____
    Suite 202   _____
    Lincoln, NE 68510

☐ Charge my credit card
    ☐ Visa   ☐ MasterCard
Account #_____
Exp. Date _____
Signature _____
Phone # _____